The Crêpe Cookbook

The Crêpe Cookbook

Anne Marshall

 CHARTWELL BOOKS INC.

Published by Chartwell Books Inc.
A Division of Book Sales Inc.
110 Enterprise Avenue
Secaucus, New Jersey 07094

Acknowledgments

My warmest thanks to Susan Donaldson for her assistance in testing the recipes in this book, to Judy Bokor for her accuracy in typing the manuscript, to Norman Nicholls for his artistry in photographing the pictures for this book and to Snape & Gallaher Graphics, the designers, for putting it all together so attractively.

My sincere thanks to the following for their kind co-operation and generosity:

The Bay Tree for French steel crêpe pans in photograph of equipment; round copper dish in French Chicken Crêpes and Blini; green and white pottery in Apple Pancakes Longueville.

Giftmaker for upside-down crêpe pan, griddle, chicken and apron in photograph of equipment; tray and round white plates in Blini; cruet in Chicken Paprika with Pancakes; bamboo tray in Spring Rolls and Won Tons; Mexican pottery in Acapulco Enchiladas; blue and white china in Swiss Pancakes.

Josiah Wedgwood and Sons Australia Pty Ltd for pottery in Ham Strudel and Mushroom Sauce; china in Wholemeal Spinach Pancakes with Tomato Sauce; white hexagonal plate in Christmas Crêpes; white plates in Jubilee Crêpes; blue and white plate and bowl in Strawberry Pancake Gâteau.

Monier Consumer Products for a Monier electric crêpe maker.

This edition
Published by Chartwell Books Inc.
A Division of Book Sales Inc.
110 Enterprise Avenue
Secaucus, New Jersey 07094

First published by Paul Hamlyn Pty Limited
176 South Creek Road, Dee Why West, Australia 2099
First published 1977
© Copyright Paul Hamlyn Pty Limited
Produced in Australia by the Publisher
Typeset in Australia by G.T. Setters Pty Limited
Printed by Tien Wah Press (PTE) Ltd.,
977 Bukit Timah Road, Singapore 21
ISBN: 0-89009-308-3

Contents

Introduction

More and more people are enjoying crêpes these days. Crêpe is the French word for a paper-thin, lacy pancake. The family pancake has been made by cooks for years and years, but the crêpe rose to the level of *haute cuisine* in elegant restaurants around the world. Now, we have restaurants specialising in crêpes and pancakes only, and their menus illustrate clearly how versatile and relatively economical they are.

The Crêpe Cookbook invites you to experiment with crêpe dishes at home in your own kitchen. I have given you a variety of batter recipes to use—all you need for the many and varied internationally inspired recipes which follow. There is also sound information on cooking in crêpe pans and on the new upside-down crêpe pans as well as cooking on the equally new automatic crêpe maker.

Once you have prepared your crêpes there is an endless variety of fillings to choose from, delicious savoury ones with rich sauces or sweet ones laced with liqueur.

There are crêpes from around the world, the ever popular Chinese Spring Rolls, Blini and Enchiladas to quote a few. Then there are some griddle cakes for breakfast and afternoon tea.

You can now see how versatile crêpes and pancakes are. I hope this little book will help you to enjoy both making and sharing many delicious crêpe dishes.

ANNE E. MARSHALL

Weights and Measures

All the recipes in this book use metric weights and measures in accordance with the Standards Association of Australia.

A reliable set of metric scales, a set of Australian Standard measuring cups (1, ½, ⅓, ¼, cup), a set of Australian Standard measuring spoons (1 tablespoon, 1 teaspoon, ½ teaspoon, ¼ teaspoon), a 1 litre graduated measuring jug and a 250 ml graduated jug are necessary equipment for successful metric cookery. Some, but not all, of this equipment is essential. It is all available at leading kitchenware and hardware shops.

The Australian Standard measuring cup has a capacity of 250 millilitres (250 ml).

The Australian Standard tablespoon has a capacity of 20 millilitres (20 ml).

The Australian Standard teaspoon has a capacity of 5 millilitres (5 ml).

In certain recipes, some imperial weights are given in brackets as a shopping guide, e.g., meat, fish, fruit, vegetables, chocolate, where it is either impossible to buy in metric weights or where it is impractical to measure in a cup.

Temperatures are given in metric with imperial temperatures in brackets.

Measurements of length are given in metric with imperial measurements in brackets.

Important point: New Zealand, American and Canadian weights and measures are the same except that the Australian Standard measuring tablespoon has a capacity of 20 millilitres (20 ml), whereas the New Zealand, American and Canadian Standard measuring tablespoon has a capacity of 15 millilitres (15 ml).

In Britain, 1 ounce has been rounded down to a metric conversion of 25 grams, whereas in Australia, 1 ounce has been rounded up to a metric conversion of 30 grams. It is therefore important that cooks in Britain follow the metric weights and measures most accurately in this cookbook.

A SPECIAL NOTE TO NORTH AMERICAN READERS

Lists of ingredients in this book have been designed to cater for cooks using either American Standard measures or metric measures, as can be seen from the following example:

> 1.5 kg (3 lb) chicken
> 3 cups water
> 2 large onions
> 5 tablespoons flour
> ½ cup milk

This listing can be read in two ways:

American	Metric
3 pound chicken	1.5 kilogram chicken
3 AMERICAN cups water	3 METRIC cups water
2 large onions	2 large onions
5 AMERICAN tablespoons flour	5 METRIC tablespoons flour
½ AMERICAN cup milk	½ AMERICAN cup milk

It must be stresssed that the quantities given in the American and metric ingredients listings are in proportion, but they are NOT exact conversions — the metric yield is approximately 10 per cent greater than the equivalent American Standard yield. Therefore, to use this book successfully, follow American Standard quantities **or** follow metric quantities **but do not** use a mixture of the two.

Using metric measures
The metric measuring cup specified in this book has a capacity of **250 millilitres** (250 ml). Clearly graduated metric measuring cups and jugs can therefore be used for all liquid and dry cup quantities given in the recipes. Note that:

¼ metric cup	=	60 ml
½ metric cup	=	125 ml
¾ metric cup	=	185 ml
1 metric cup	=	250 ml = ¼ litre
2 metric cups	=	500 ml = ½ litre
3 metric cups	=	750 ml = ¾ litre
4 metric cups	=	1,000 ml = 1 litre

The American Standard teaspoon and tablespoon can be used for measuring metric quantities. The American teaspoon has exactly the same capacity as the metric teaspoon specified in this book:

1 metric teaspoon = 5 ml = 1 American teaspoon

IMPORTANT POINTS
New Zealand, Canadian and **American** weights and measures are the same except that the Australian Standard measuring tablespoon has a capacity of 20 millilitres (20 ml) or 4 teaspoons, whereas the New Zealand, Canadian and American Standard measuring tablespoons have a capacity of 15 millilitres (15 ml) or 3 teaspoons.

American/British Consumer Guide

Even though we all speak the same English language in Australia, America and Britain, the terminology for certain cooking ingredients and methods differs, so I am including this brief guide to help clear up any confusion.

Australia	America	Britain
baking powder	baking soda	baking powder
cream	light cream	single cream
thickened cream	heavy cream	double cream
cornflour	cornstarch	cornflour
minced beef	ground beef	minced beef
pawpaw	papaya	paw paw
green banana peppers	green banana peppers	green Hungarian peppers
plain flour	all purpose flour	plain flour
prawns	shrimps	prawns
king prawns	large shrimps	scampi
shallots	green onions/eschallots	spring onions
sour cream	dairy sour cream	soured cream
stock cube	bouillon cube	stock cube
sugar	sugar	granulated sugar
caster sugar	sugar	caster sugar
icing sugar	confectioner's sugar	icing sugar
tomato paste	tomato paste	tomato purée
finely chopped	minced	finely chopped
grill	broil	grill

Crêpe Pans

French crêpe pans

If you want to master the skill of crêpe making, a good crêpe pan is an essential investment. Practice makes perfect and, if you look after your crêpe pan properly, your crêpes will be thin and lacy and will never stick. You will soon be tossing them confidently around the kitchen to the delight of your family and guests.

The traditional crêpe pan is a French steel pan. It has been around for years and is available in most specialty kitchenware stores. The best sizes are 15–18 cm (6–7 inch) diameter crêpe pans, although a wide range of sizes is available, as shown in the picture of equipment (page 1). The French crêpe pan has sloping sides which make it easy to turn the crêpes over and to slide them out.

A new crêpe pan may have a protective coating on it. If so, remove it by rubbing with a wad of paper towels soaked in methylated spirits or soak in hot soapy water and methylated spirits, then scrub with an abrasive soap pad or an abrasive and fine steel wool and finally wash out well. It also must be 'seasoned' before use. Place a little oil or unsalted butter or white shortening and salt in the pan and heat until quite hot then wipe clean with a wad of absorbent kitchen paper.

Never wash the pan as this will cause the crêpes to stick. Clean it by 'seasoning' and then wrap the pan in greaseproof paper and store in a sealed plastic bag.

Other pans

Do not be put off crêpe making for want of a proper pan. A small cast iron or heavy-based stainless steel frying pan or an aluminium or non-stick coated frying pan can be used. Season the pan as directed to prevent the crêpes from sticking and remember that the first crêpe is always a practice one.

Upside-down crêpe pans

Upside-down crêpe pans are cleverly designed. The flat, raised cooking surface is heated, then dipped into a round shallow plate of batter. The batter sticks in a thin layer to the hot metal and the pan is then turned over and placed over the heat until the crêpe is cooked. The crêpe peels off the pan when it is turned over. Upside-down pans have to be well oiled before use and stored as for French crêpe pans.

Automatic crêpe maker

The electric automatic crêpe maker works on the same principle as the upside-down crêpe pan but has the advantage of being automatically controlled. The non-stick Teflon surface must be well rubbed or brushed with clean oil before use to prevent the crêpes from sticking.

Crêpe Batters

No one is quite sure who made the first crêpe but it probably all started centuries ago when someone made a simple flour and water batter and cooked it on a flat hot stone over a fire. In fact, in the small country of Wales, the griddle is still referred to as a 'bak'stone' (bake-stone) and in old English recipe books pancakes are called hearth cakes.

The most popular batters today are the Basic Pancake batter and the French Crêpe batter, the latter being a little richer. A basic batter is a mixture of flour, eggs, milk and butter or oil or cream. The butter, oil or cream is added to give richness and to prevent the crêpes from sticking during cooking. Sugar, liqueur or chopped nuts may be added to a batter which is to be used for dessert crêpes.

For those interested in nutritional values try the wholemeal crêpes, or substitute wheatgerm for a quarter of the flour in the basic batter, or use natural yoghurt or buttermilk in place of the milk. Other batters contain ground buckwheat in place of flour and some traditional pancakes are made from a yeast batter.

For a lighter batter, try adding a little soda water in place of the liquid or fold in whisked egg white for a dessert crêpe.

Most of these batters can be successfully made in a blender or in a food processor but they are all easy to make in a mixing bowl with a wooden spoon. It's just a matter of beating well (with the back of the spoon) to get rid of all the lumps.

When the batter is mixed to a smooth consistency, cover it and leave it to stand for an hour, if possible, before cooking. Letting it stand allows the starch grains to soften, thus giving you a tender crêpe. Stand the mixture in the refrigerator on a hot day.

Basic Pancakes

Makes approx 12 pancakes

---

125 g (1 cup) plain or all-purpose flour
pinch of salt
1 large egg
1 egg yolk
300 ml (approx 1¼ cups) milk
1 tablespoon melted butter
1 tablespoon cream, optional
unsalted butter or lard or white vegetable shortening for cooking

Sift flour and salt into a mixing bowl and make a well in the centre. Add egg and egg yolk and a little milk and stir in centre of bowl with a wooden spoon, working a little flour into the liquid.

Gradually add half the milk, mixing continuously until all the flour is worked into the liquid, then beat with the back of the wooden spoon until smooth and free from lumps. Stir in the melted butter and cream then add the remaining milk.

Cover and leave to stand for 30 minutes–1 hour in order to soften the starch grains and give a lighter pancake.

Note: Use unsalted butter for cooking pancakes which are to be used for dessert crêpes, but use either unsalted butter or lard or white vegetable shortening for cooking pancakes which are to be used for savoury crêpes.

French Crêpes

Makes approx 16 crêpes

---

155 g (1¼ cups) plain or all-purpose flour
½ teaspoon salt
3 large eggs
250 ml (1 cup) milk
4 tablespoons water
45 g (1½ tablespoons) melted unsalted butter
extra 45 g (1½ tablespoons) melted unsalted butter
mixed with 1 tablespoon oil for cooking

Sift flour and salt into a mixing bowl and make a well in the centre. Add eggs and beat in the surrounding flour with the back of a wooden spoon. When egg mixture starts to thicken, gradually add half the milk and beat well until batter is smooth.

Stir in remaining milk and water, then sieve batter through a fine sieve into another bowl and add 45 g melted butter. Cover bowl and chill in refrigerator for 1–2 hours before use.

Note: This batter may be mixed in a blender or food processor. Mix all ingredients for a few seconds, turn machine off, scrape down sides and bottom of blender or food processor with a plastic spatula, then mix again for a further 40 seconds.

American Crêpe Batter
Makes 12–14 crêpes

3 large eggs
185 ml (¾ cup) milk
60 g (¼ cup) melted butter or margarine
90 g (¾ cup) plain or all-purpose flour, sifted
¼ teaspoon salt

Combine all ingredients and whirl in a blender for about 30 seconds. Scrape down any flour adhering to the sides with a plastic spatula and whirl for another 5 seconds. (Or combine ingredients and beat with an electric or rotary hand mixer until smooth.)

Cover and refrigerate for at least 1 hour. Before using, add more milk if necessary to bring batter to the consistency of fresh cream. If too thin add 1 or 2 tablespoons extra flour to thicken to the correct consistency.

Big Batch Pancakes
Makes 40 × 20 cm (8 inch) pancakes or
50 × 18 cm (7 inch) pancakes

750 g (6 cups) plain or all-purpose flour
2 pinches salt
3 large eggs
1.2 litres (2 bottles) milk
unsalted butter, oil or vegetable shortening for cooking

Sift flour and salt into a large mixing bowl. Make a well in the centre of the flour with a wooden spoon, add the eggs and beat well, gradually working in the flour from the sides.

When egg mixture starts to thicken in centre of bowl, add the milk gradually and beat well until the batter is smooth.

Cook pancakes in the normal way.

Cornmeal Crêpes

Makes approx 12 crêpes

90 g (½ cup) cornmeal
125 ml (½ cup) boiling water
3 large eggs
60 g (½ cup) plain or all-purpose flour
½ teaspoon salt
60 g (2 tablespoons) melted butter or margarine
185 ml (¾ cup) milk

Place cornmeal in a mixing bowl, pour boiling water over and stir with a wooden spoon until smooth. Cool slightly.

Gradually add eggs, sifted flour and salt, beating after each addition until smooth. Stir in melted butter and milk.

Cover batter and allow to stand for 1 hour before use. Stir batter occasionally throughout the cooking process to keep it smooth. Cooks particularly well on an automatic crêpe maker.

Note: Cornmeal Crêpes may be substituted for tortillas in enchilada recipes but the frying in oil/lard/shortening process should be omitted. Simply dip crêpes in the sauce, then fill, roll and bake as directed in the recipe.

Spring Roll Pancakes

Makes approx 12 pancakes

---

250 g (2 cups) plain or all-purpose flour
½ teaspoon salt
2 large eggs
375 ml (1½ cups) water
lard for frying

Sift flour and salt into a mixing bowl. Make a well in the centre, add eggs and beat with a wooden spoon, gradually working in the flour from around the sides. Add water and beat well until mixture is smooth and free from lumps.

Allow batter to stand for 1 hour before cooking. Cook in a 15 cm (6 inch) crêpe pan in a little lard as directed.

Pour the pancake batter into a 250 ml (1 cup) measuring jug and pour about 60 ml (¼ cup) of the batter into the crêpe pan, moving it around quickly so that the batter covers the base of the pan. Cook for ½ minute, then gently loosen edges with a palette knife and cook for a further 2 minutes, shaking the pan frequently. Turn or toss pancake over and cook the other side for ½ minute.

Slide cooked pancake out on to an enamel plate. Continue making pancakes in this way until all the batter is used. Allow to cool before filling.

Wholemeal Pancakes

Makes approx 12 pancakes

125 g (1 cup) finely ground wholemeal flour
30 g (1 tablespoon) melted butter or polyunsaturated margarine
3 large eggs
300 ml (approx 1¼ cups) milk
unsalted butter, lard or white shortening for cooking

To make batter: Place wholemeal flour in a mixing bowl and make a well in the centre. Add melted butter, eggs and half the milk and beat with the back of a wooden spoon until smooth. Stir in the remaining milk.

Cover batter and leave to stand for 30 minutes.

To cook pancakes: Season a 16.5 cm (6½ inch) crêpe pan by melting a knob of unsalted butter in it over a medium-high heat (no. 7 on an electric hotplate), then rubbing it clean with a wad of kitchen paper.

Melt approximately 1 teaspoon unsalted butter in the seasoned pan over a medium-high heat, pour in approximately ¼ cup batter and tilt the pan quickly until the batter coats the bottom in a thin layer. Cook pancake until golden brown underneath, shaking pan occasionally to loosen pancake, then turn over with a palette knife, or toss over, and cook other side until golden brown.

Slide pancake out on to a heatproof plate and place a strip of greaseproof paper over the centre. Continue cooking and layering wholemeal pancakes, adding 1 teaspoon unsalted butter for each one, until all batter is cooked.

Cooking Crêpes

To cook crêpes/pancakes in a crêpe pan

First choose the correct pan. Use a traditional French steel crêpe pan if possible or a small, heavy-based frying pan. All the crêpes in the recipes in this book have been made in a 16.5 cm (6½ inch) crêpe pan, the most popular size, unless otherwise stated.

Place the pan over a medium heat and add a knob of unsalted (or clarified) butter or lard or white vegetable shortening. Heat well and swirl around the pan then wipe clean with a wad of absorbent kitchen paper. This is known as 'seasoning' the pan. When the pan is thoroughly cleaned and well seasoned, the crêpes/pancakes should not stick, so you can start cooking.

Heat a small knob of unsalted butter or lard or shortening in the pan or a teaspoon of melted unsalted butter mixed with oil (see French Crêpes recipe), then add a large cooking spoon of batter or two metal tablespoons of batter and, working quickly, twist the pan clockwise so that the batter quickly coats the whole base of the pan and sets in a complete round.

Cook over a medium-high heat (no. 7 electric), shaking the pan occasionally to loosen the crêpe/pancake. When it is golden brown underneath, toss the crêpe over or flip over with a palette knife. Cook other side until golden brown.

When cooked, slide crêpe out opposite handle of pan on to a strip of greaseproof paper on a wire cooling rack or an enamel plate.

The first crêpe is always a trial one to test the temperature, cooking time and amount of batter to use.

Continue cooking crêpes in this method, stacking them with strips of greaseproof paper between them to prevent sticking, until all batter is cooked.

Wipe pan clean with a wad of kitchen paper—do not wash it—and keep it for making crêpes/pancakes only.

To cook on an upside-down crêpe pan

If using an upside-down crêpe pan the method is as follows:

Pour the prepared batter into a round shallow tart plate.

Apply a light coating of vegetable oil over the cooking surface of the pan, using a paper towel or greasing brush. Set the pan over a gas burner or an electric hot plate at medium-high heat until the pan takes on a dark brown colour.

Let the pan cool a few minutes, then recoat lightly with oil. Again heat the pan until it darkens a little more. Your crêpe pan is now seasoned and ready for cooking. Proper seasoning is a guarantee that crêpes will never stick to the pan.

Turn the hot upside-down crêpe pan over and dip the top of the pan evenly into the batter (about 6 mm/¼ inch deep) and lift straight up immediately to obtain an even coating. (If the coating of batter is too thin or if you want a thicker crêpe, dip the griddle into the batter a second time.)

　　　　Wholemeal Spinach Pancakes with Tomato Sauce

Cook the crêpe by turning the pan over and placing it, crêpe-side up, over the heat. Cook until the edges turn a golden brown. The crêpes are cooked only on one side.

Invert the pan over a large plate and the crêpe should slide off on to it. If it tends to stick, loosen the edges with a round-bladed knife and ease the crêpe from the pan.

Continue cooking crêpes in this method, layering them with strips of greaseproof paper in between, until all the batter is cooked.

To remove any crumbs from the pan during cooking, wipe the pan lightly with the oil-moistened paper towel or a greasing brush dipped in oil.

Wipe pan clean with a wad of kitchen paper—do not wash it—and keep it for making crêpes/pancakes only.

To cook on an automatic crêpe maker

The automatic crêpe maker is a magic electric pan which cooks crêpes upside down.

Before using for the first time, wipe the non-stick Teflon surface with a wad of paper towels soaked in vegetable oil, melted white shortening or unsalted butter to 'season' it and prevent the crêpes from sticking.

Pour the batter into a round, shallow tart plate slightly larger than the crêpe maker.

Heat the crêpe maker until the light on the handle goes on; this indicates it is hot enough to cook a crêpe. Invert the crêpe maker and dip it into the batter for about 3 seconds, until it is coated with a thin layer.

Remove from the batter, turn over (the light will have gone off) and allow to stand until the light goes on again. The crêpe should have stopped steaming and should be slightly browned around the edge. The crêpes are cooked on one side only.

Turn the crêpe maker and hold it over a flat plate, loosen the edge of the crêpe with a plastic spatula and the crêpe will drop off on to the plate.

Continue making crêpes in this way, using the light as a dipping and cooking guide, and stack them with strips of greaseproof paper in between.

If the crêpes stick, wipe the surface of the crêpe maker with a little more oil between each dipping.

Heating, Storing and Freezing

To keep crêpes hot

Stack the crêpes straight from the pan, as they are cooked, on an enamel plate, layered with strips of greaseproof paper between them, as directed in the section on cooking crêpes (page 18). Have the plate ready over a large pan of simmering water and keep the crêpes covered with the lid of the pan or with aluminium foil, so that they keep hot. The hot crêpes may then be filled with a hot filling and 'flashed' under a hot grill and served at once.

To store crêpes

Crêpes may be stored for a few days in the refrigerator without freezing. Cook and stack them as directed, then place in an airtight plastic container and store in refrigerator. Use within three days to retain a good texture.

To freeze crêpes

To freeze crêpes, stack as directed, wrap securely in a plastic bag or foil or pack in an airtight plastic container. Don't forget to label with name, quantity and date of freezing. Alternatively, fill crêpes with filling, roll up or fold into quarters and pack into a buttered, ovenproof, freezer-proof dish and cover with foil or pack dish into a plastic bag, seal well and freeze.

To reheat frozen crêpes

If crêpes are not filled, place the stack (with paper strips) on an ovenproof plate, cover with foil and place in a slow oven until thawed, then fill, heat through and serve as required.

If crêpes are already filled when frozen, reheat in the buttered, ovenproof, freezer-proof dish in which they are packed, in a moderate oven.

Folding and Flaming

To fold crêpes

Crêpes may be folded in various ways. Shape them with the more attractive side on the outside. Those cooked in a traditional crêpe pan are always better looking on the side which is cooked first. Those made on upside-down pans or on an electric crêpe maker are browned on one side only, the side which cooked against the pan.

Rolled crêpes

Spread the filling over the lower half of the crêpe and roll up like a Swiss roll.

Folded crêpes

Place filling in the centre of the crêpe, fold in half, then fold in half again, forming a triangle four layers thick. This method is good for thin fillings and is often known as the Crêpe Suzette fold.

Fold-over crêpes

Place filling along the centre of the crêpe, fold one side over to cover filling, then fold the other side over to overlap the first fold. This method is good for thick fillings.

Spring roll fold

Spread filling to within 1 cm (½ inch) of edge. Fold sides of crêpe over filling, then roll up from bottom to top. This shape is good if the filled crêpes are to be deep fried.

Blintz fold

Spoon filling into centre of crêpe, fold bottom over half the filling, fold left side over filling, fold right side over to overlap left side, then fold top down to enclose filling. This is often known as the envelope fold.

Stacked crêpes

Place crêpes, best side up, on a flat serving plate and spread nearly to edge with filling. Continue layering crêpes with filling to desired height. Serve cut in wedges.

To flame crêpes

Crêpes are flamed or flambéed both for effect and for flavour. Any overproof brandy, cognac, rum or liqueur may be used. The most popular liqueurs are Grand Marnier, Cointreau, orange curaçao and kirsch.

The art of flaming is simple. The secret is that both the crêpes and the spirit or liqueur must be hot in order to ignite. The spirit or liqueur may be added to the pan of hot crêpes over a spirit burner and heated gently or it may be heated in a separate pan, then poured over the hot crêpes and finally ignited with a long match or taper.

Allow the flame to die out before serving and never add more spirit while the flame is burning.

Savoury Crêpes

Savoury crêpes make a magnificent entrée at a dinner party. They can also be served at a stylish breakfast buffet, for a light lunch with salad, for a main meal with rice and vegetables or for a super supper snack.

Crêpes and pancakes are a very versatile way of serving fish, meat, poultry and vegetables in attractive savoury dishes. You can concoct the most elaborate fillings, rich and delicious, healthy and wholesome. No other dish lends itself quite so much to the cook's imagination.

Seafood crêpes are particularly spectacular. The fish must be cooked first and is then combined with a rich velvety sauce, a cheese sauce or maybe a tangy tomato sauce. Canned tuna and salmon also make versatile fillings for crêpes.

Chicken is popular as a pancake filling and meat is very satisfying. A small quantity of either can be extended with a delicious sauce to fill enough crêpes to serve six to eight people. The enveloping crêpes transform the fillings to the world of *haute cuisine.*

Left-over meat is also good in a crêpe filling.

Vegetables with cheese can be the basis of a variety of delicious crêpes and combine splendidly with wholemeal pancakes.

As a guide to serves, most of the following recipes suggest the number of entrée portions, allowing 2 crêpes per portion. However, if you wish to serve them as a main course for a family meal or for a lunch or supper dish, allow 3 crêpes per portion. If you add boiled rice and green vegetables or serve them with hot bread and follow with a salad, you can turn your crêpe dishes into satisfying family meals.

24

Crayfish Crêpes

Serves 4-8

---

8 crêpes
Filling:
1 × 1 kg (2 lb) cooked crayfish
1 quantity Hollandaise Sauce
2 teaspoons chopped dill
extra chopped dill for garnish

Prepare crêpes according to French Crêpes recipe (page 13).

Filling: Cut crayfish in half lengthways and remove and discard intestine and coral. Remove flesh from shell and flake with a fork, removing and discarding any pieces of inner shell.

Fold flaked crayfish into Hollandaise Sauce and stir dill into the mixture.

To finish: Divide filling between the crêpes and shape in a line along the centre of each one. Roll up crêpes and arrange in a single layer in a buttered ovenproof baking dish.

Heat crêpes through in a moderately hot oven at 190°C (375°F) for 15 minutes. Serve immediately sprinkled with extra chopped dill.

Note: Lobster or king prawns may be used in place of crayfish.

Hollandaise Sauce

---

125 g (4 tablespoons) unsalted butter
4 egg yolks
2 teaspoons lemon juice
salt and pepper

Place 1 tablespoon unsalted butter and 4 egg yolks in the top of a double-boiler. Place over hot, but not boiling, water, stir quickly and constantly until sauce is well combined. Slowly add remaining butter, whisking the mixture constantly until sauce is well mixed and thickened.

Remove top of double-boiler from heat and beat sauce well for 2 minutes. Add lemon juice, salt and pepper to taste and place over hot water and beat for a further 2 minutes.

Crêpes St Jacques
Serves 6

12 crêpes/pancakes
Filling:
500 g (1 lb) scallops
30 g (2 tablespoons) plain or all-purpose flour
60 g (2 tablespoons) butter
½ cup thinly sliced shallots
1 small clove garlic, crushed
3 tablespoons brown breadcrumbs
1 teaspoon salt
¼ teaspoon white pepper
125 ml (½ cup) dry white wine
2 tablespoons chopped parsley
lemon wedges for serving

Make crêpes as in French Crêpes recipe (page 13).

Filling: Cut scallops into 1 cm (½ inch) cubes and coat them with the flour.

Heat butter in a saucepan and gently fry shallots and garlic for 5 minutes or until soft and golden. Add scallops, breadcrumbs, salt and pepper and cook gently for 5 minutes, stirring frequently.

Add wine and parsley, bring to the boil, then cover and simmer gently for 5 minutes.

To finish: Divide filling between crêpes and fold sides over. Place filled crêpes in a single layer in a buttered, shallow baking dish and heat through in a moderately hot oven at 190°C (375°F) for 10–15 minutes.

Serve immediately with lemon wedges.

Crispy Crab Crêpes
Serves 6

12 crêpes/pancakes
Filling:
500 g (2 cups) crab meat, fresh or canned
1 egg, beaten
½ teaspoon salt
¼ teaspoon white pepper
2 tablespoons mayonnaise
1 tablespoon brandy or cognac
beaten egg for glazing
Coating:
1 egg, beaten
2 tablespoons milk
125 g (1 cup) dry breadcrumbs
or cornflake crumbs
oil for deep frying

Prepare crêpes according to French Crêpes recipe or pancakes according to Basic Pancakes recipe (page 13).

Filling: Combine crab meat, beaten egg, salt, pepper, mayonnaise and brandy in a mixing bowl.

To finish: Place approximately 2 tablespoons crab filling in the centre of each crêpe. Roll the crêpes into tight rolls, glazing the edge of each with some beaten egg so that they are well sealed.

Coating: Beat egg and milk together in a shallow bowl. Dip one crêpe at a time into the mixture, then roll in breadcrumbs.

If you do not wish to cook the crêpes immediately, store uncovered in the refrigerator until ready to cook.

Heat oil to 190ºC (375ºF) in a deep fryer or a heavy, deep pan. Deep fry the crêpes, being careful not to overcrowd the pan, for 1 minute on each side. Remove and drain on absorbent kitchen paper or paper towels. Serve at once with tartare sauce.

Prawn Pancakes

Serves 6

12 pancakes/crêpes
Filling:
500 ml (2 cups) Béchamel Sauce
lemon juice to taste
2 teaspoons chopped parsley
500 g (1 lb) small prawns, shelled and deveined
2 tablespoons cream
1 tablespoon grated Parmesan cheese
parsley sprigs and lemon wedges for garnish

Make pancakes as directed for Basic Pancakes or crêpes as for French Crêpes (page 13).

Filling: Prepare Béchamel Sauce as directed in recipe and add lemon juice to taste. Remove 60 ml (¼ cup) of sauce and reserve. Stir chopped parsley and prawns into remainder and heat without boiling.

To finish: Place 1 tablespoon hot prawn filling in a line on each pancake and roll it up into a cigar shape. Keep warm in an ovenproof dish in a low oven.

Stir cream into the reserved sauce and pour over pancakes. Sprinkle Parmesan cheese over the top and place under a medium-hot grill for 5 minutes.

Serve hot, garnished with a sprig of parsley and lemon wedges.

Béchamel Sauce

Makes 500 ml (2 cups)

500 ml (2 cups) milk
1 onion, coarsely chopped
1 carrot, coarsely chopped
1 stalk celery, coarsely chopped
1 bouquet garni
45 g (1½ tablespoons) butter
45 g (3 tablespoons) plain or all-purpose flour
salt
white pepper

Place milk in the top of a double-boiler with onion, carrot, celery and bouquet garni. Cover and heat over simmering water for 30 minutes to allow milk to absorb flavours. Strain off milk.

Melt butter in a saucepan, stir in flour and cook roux over a medium heat for 1–2 minutes, stirring continuously or until the roux 'honeycombs' (looks foamy and granular).

Remove saucepan from heat, cool slightly and stir in the warm milk gradually, beating and stirring with a wooden spoon until smooth.

Bring sauce to the boil, stirring continuously, then simmer for 1 minute. Season to taste with salt and pepper.

Salmon and Cucumber Pancakes
Serves 6

12 pancakes
Filling:
60 g (2 tablespoons) soft butter or polyunsaturated margarine
60 g (4 tablespoons) plain or all-purpose flour
600 ml (approx 2½ cups) milk
salt and white pepper
1 × 425 g (14 oz) can salmon
6 shallots, thinly sliced
½ cup finely chopped cucumber
4 tablespoons natural yoghurt
60 g (½ cup) grated Cheddar cheese

Make pancakes according to Basic Pancakes recipe (page 13).

Filling: Place soft butter, flour and milk in a saucepan and bring to the boil over a medium heat, whisking continuously with a balloon-shaped wire whisk. Simmer for 1 minute, then season to taste with salt and pepper.

Place salmon and juice on a plate, remove skin and bones and flake the salmon. Stir salmon and juice, onion, cucumber and yoghurt into half the sauce.

To finish: Divide the filling between the pancakes and roll them up. Place stuffed pancakes in a buttered, ovenproof serving dish, coat with remaining sauce and sprinkle with cheese. Bake in a hot oven at 200⁰C (400⁰F) for 10–15 minutes, until bubbling hot. Serve immediately.

Smoked Salmon Crêpes

Serves 4-8

8 crêpes
Filling:
125 g (4 oz) thinly sliced smoked salmon
2 hard-boiled eggs
2 teaspoons chopped capers
2 teaspoons chopped chives
185 ml (¾ cup) Mayonnaise
lemon wedges for serving

Prepare crêpes according to French Crêpes recipe (page 13).

Filling: Trim salmon and cut into short julienne strips. Shell hard-boiled eggs while still warm and chop coarsely.

Mix salmon, eggs, capers and chives into Mayonnaise.

To finish: Divide filling between the crêpes and roll them up. Place in a buttered ovenproof dish and heat in a moderate oven at 180ºC (350ºF) for 15 minutes.

Serve hot with lemon wedges.

Mayonnaise

Makes approx 185 ml (¾ cup)

2 egg yolks
1 teaspoon white wine vinegar
½ teaspoon salt
½ teaspoon mustard powder
pinch of white pepper
150 ml (⅝ cup) olive oil
few drops lemon juice

Place egg yolks, white wine vinegar, salt, mustard and pepper in the small bowl of an electric mixer, and beat until combined. Add olive oil, drop by drop, beating at medium speed all the time, until approximately 2 tablespoons have been added.

Add a few drops of lemon juice to bring mixture to the consistency of cream. Add the remaining oil in a thin, steady stream, beating continuously, stopping the addition of oil from time to time to make sure the mixture is combining well.

When all the oil has been added and the mayonnaise is thick, add extra lemon juice to taste and adjust seasoning.

When completed, the mayonnaise should be thick enough to keep its shape.

Trout Pancakes

Serves 6–8

12–16 pancakes/crêpes
Filling:
6 fillets cooked trout
½ quantity Velouté Sauce (page 40)
2 teaspoons horseradish sauce
salt and pepper
squeeze of lemon juice
grated Parmesan cheese for sprinkling
parsley sprigs for garnish
lemon wedges for serving

Prepare batter and make pancakes as directed in Basic Pancakes recipe or crêpes according to French Crêpes recipe (page 13).

Filling: Cook trout fillets by steaming in a little white wine. Remove skin from trout and flake fish with a fork. Mix fish with Velouté Sauce, horseradish sauce, salt and pepper and lemon juice to taste.

To finish: Spread filling over pancakes and roll up into cigar shapes. Place in a buttered baking dish and sprinkle with Parmesan cheese. Bake in a moderately hot oven at 190°C (375°F) for 10–15 minutes or until piping hot.

Serve immediately garnished with parsley and accompanied with lemon wedges.

Note: Ask your fishman for heads and bones from filleted trout and use to make a strong fish stock for the Velouté Sauce.

Tuna Pancakes

Serves 6

12 pancakes
Filling:
2 stalks celery, thinly sliced
30 g (1 tablespoon) soft butter or margarine
30 g (2 tablespoons) plain or all-purpose flour
300 ml (approx 1¼ cups) milk
2 tablespoons chopped red pepper
60 g (½ cup) Cheddar cheese, grated
1 × 425 g (14 oz) can tuna fish, drained and flaked
salt and pepper
parsley sprigs for garnish

Make pancakes according to recipe for Basic Pancakes (page 13).

Filling: Place celery in boiling water in a small pan. Cover and boil for 8 minutes, drain well.

Place butter or margarine, flour and milk together in a heavy-based saucepan and bring to the boil over a medium heat, whisking continuously with a wire balloon-shaped whisk. Reduce heat and simmer for 1 minute.

Stir celery, red pepper and grated cheese into sauce and heat until cheese melts. Fold flaked tuna into sauce and season to taste with salt and pepper.

To finish: Spread hot tuna filling over top half of each pancake, fold bottom over then fold one side over to meet other side, forming a triangle. Place filled pancakes in a buttered, shallow, ovenproof serving dish.

Heat pancakes in a moderately hot oven at 190ºC (375ºF) for 15 minutes or until heated through. Serve hot, garnished with parsley sprigs.

Brain Crêpes
Serves 6

1 quantity crêpes/pancakes
Filling:
750 g (1½ lb) calves' or lambs' brains
30 g (2 tablespoons) plain or all-purpose flour
125 g (½ cup) butter or polyunsaturated margarine
¼ cup sliced shallots
1 teaspoon salt
¼ teaspoon pepper
rind and juice of 1 lemon
¼ cup chopped parsley
60 ml (¼ cup) white wine
lemon wedges for serving

Prepare crêpes as directed in French Crêpes recipe or pancakes as in Basic Pancakes recipe (page 13).

Filling: Soak brains in cold salted water for 30 minutes then drain and remove transparent skin. Cut brains into 2.5 cm (1 inch) pieces, then roll in flour until well coated.

Heat butter or margarine in a frying pan and gently fry brains and shallots for 10 minutes, stirring frequently. Drain off excess fat. Add salt, pepper, lemon rind and juice, parsley and wine to pan and simmer for 5 minutes to reduce liquid.

To finish: Divide filling between crêpes, roll up neatly and place in a shallow, buttered baking dish. Place in a moderate oven at 180⁰C (350⁰F) for 15 minutes or until heated through.

Serve immediately with lemon wedges.

Asparagus and Ham Crêpes

Serves 6

---

12 crêpes/pancakes
Filling:
60 g (2 tablespoons) soft butter or margarine
30 g (2 tablespoons) plain or all-purpose flour
250 ml (1 cup) milk
250 g (8 oz) cooked ham, chopped
125 g (1 cup) Swiss cheese, grated
½ teaspoon salt
¼ teaspoon pepper
2 × 310 g (10 oz) cans asparagus tips, drained

Make the crêpes as directed in French Crêpes recipe or make pancakes as directed in Basic Pancakes recipe (page 13).

Filling: Place soft butter or margarine, flour and milk together in a saucepan and bring to the boil, over a medium heat, whisking continuously with a balloon-shaped wire whisk until smooth and shiny. Remove sauce from heat and stir in the ham, Swiss cheese, salt and pepper.

To finish: Divide sauce mixture between crêpes and spread evenly. Place some asparagus tips on top and roll up crêpes.

Arrange crêpes in a buttered, ovenproof serving dish and place in a moderately hot oven at 190⁰C (375⁰F) for 10–15 minutes until heated through.

Serve crêpes immediately, accompanied with a tossed salad.

Chinese Chicken Pancakes

Serves 6

---

12 pancakes
Filling:
2 onions, finely chopped
2 stalks celery, finely chopped
½ cup finely chopped mushrooms
2 tablespoons oil
250 g (8 oz) cooked chicken, finely chopped
1 tablespoon cornflour (cornstarch)
1 tablespoon soy sauce
2 tablespoons stock or dry sherry

Make pancakes as directed in Basic Pancakes recipe (page 13).

Filling: Gently fry onion, celery and mushrooms in oil for 5–10 minutes, until golden brown. Add chicken and fry for 5 minutes. Sprinkle cornflour over, then stir in soy sauce and stock and simmer for 2 minutes.

To finish: Divide filling between pancakes, roll up and place in a shallow, greased, ovenproof serving dish. Cover with foil and place in a hot oven at 200⁰C (400⁰F) for 10–15 minutes.

Serve hot with a bowl of soy sauce.

Chicken Paprika Pancakes
Serves 6

12 pancakes
Filling:
90 g (3 tablespoons) butter or margarine
1 onion, finely chopped
2 chicken breasts (schnitzel)
2 teaspoons paprika pepper
$\frac{1}{2}$ teaspoon salt
$\frac{1}{4}$ teaspoon pepper
250 ml (1 cup) chicken stock, or use stock cubes
125 ml ($\frac{1}{2}$ carton) sour cream

Prepare pancakes as directed for Basic Pancakes recipe (page 13).

Filling: Heat butter in a heavy-based pan and fry chopped onions until golden. Add chicken and brown well on both sides. Sprinkle paprika over chicken, add salt, pepper and stock. Cover and bring to the boil, reduce heat and simmer for 30–40 minutes or until chicken is tender.

Remove chicken and leave to cool. When cold, cut into cubes.

Reduce chicken liquor to $\frac{1}{2}$ cup by boiling, remove from heat. Mix sour cream and chicken into chicken liquor.

To finish: Divide chicken filling evenly between pancakes. Roll up pancakes and place in a buttered, ovenproof baking dish. Place in a moderately hot oven at 190⁰C (375⁰F) for 10–15 minutes.

Serve immediately accompanied with a green salad.

Chicken Liver Crêpes
Serves 6

12 crêpes/pancakes
Filling:
60 g (2 tablespoons) butter
2 onions, finely chopped
2 cloves garlic, crushed
250 g (8 oz) chicken livers, coarsely chopped
6 rashers bacon, rinded and chopped
1 cup finely chopped mushrooms
½ cup finely chopped parsley
1 × 425 (14 oz) can tomatoes, drained
3 tablespoons red wine
salt
freshly ground black pepper

Prepare crêpes as for French Crêpes or pancakes as for Basic Pancakes (page 13).

Filling: Heat butter in a large frying pan and gently fry onion and garlic until golden.

Add chicken livers and gently fry for a further 5 minutes. Add bacon and mushrooms and cook gently for 10 minutes.

Add chopped parsley, tomatoes, wine, salt and pepper to taste and simmer, uncovered, stirring occasionally, for 30 minutes or until thickened.

To finish: Divide filling between crêpes and roll up or fold into quarters. Place in a buttered, shallow baking dish and place in a moderately hot oven at 190°C (375°F) for 15 minutes or until heated through.

Serve immediately.

Ham Strudel with Mushroom Sauce

French Chicken Crêpes
Serves 8

---

16 French crêpes
Filling:
250 g (8 oz) mushrooms, finely chopped
60 g (2 tablespoons) butter
2 tablespoons finely chopped shallots
1 teaspoon finely snipped chives
½ teaspoon salt
freshly ground black pepper
250 g (8 oz) chicken breast, fried in 30 g (1 tablespoon) butter
1 × 425 g (14 oz) can artichoke hearts
1 teaspoon chopped parsley
600 ml (approx 2½ cups) Velouté Sauce (page 40)
juice of ½ lemon
250 ml (1 cup) cream
125 g (1 cup) finely grated Parmesan or Swiss cheese

Prepare French Crêpes as described in recipe (page 13).

Filling: Place chopped mushrooms in a square of muslin or the corner of a clean tea towel and squeeze tightly to extract as much juice as possible.

Heat butter in a frying pan and gently fry shallots for 1 minute, until soft but not brown. Stir in mushrooms and cook, stirring frequently, for 10–15 minutes or until all mushroom moisture has evaporated. Remove from heat and stir in chives, salt and pepper to taste.

Chop chicken breast finely and place in a bowl. Drain artichoke hearts, chop 2 finely and add to chicken. Reserve remainder for garnish. Add mushroom mixture, parsley, 4 tablespoons Velouté Sauce and lemon juice to chicken, mix well and adjust seasoning to taste.

To finish: Place 2 tablespoons filling on bottom half of each crêpe and roll up into a cigar shape.

Stir cream into remaining Velouté Sauce until smooth. Pour a thin layer of sauce over the bottom of a buttered, ovenproof serving dish. Arrange crêpes side by side, in 2 layers, in the dish and pour remaining sauce over the top.

Sprinkle with cheese and bake in a hot oven at 200⁰C (400⁰F) for 10–15 minutes or until golden brown and bubbling hot.

Serve immediately, garnished with slices of reserved artichoke hearts.

Velouté Sauce

Makes approx 850 ml (about 3½ cups)

90 g (3 tablespoons) butter
60 g (4 tablespoons) plain or all-purpose flour
600 ml (approx 2½ cups) chicken stock
2 egg yolks
250 ml (1 cup) cream
1 teaspoon salt
¼ teaspoon white pepper
1 teaspoon lemon juice

Melt butter in a saucepan, then stir in the flour and cook the roux over a medium heat for 1–2 minutes, stirring continuously, until the roux 'honeycombs' (looks foamy and granular).

Remove saucepan from heat, then gradually beat in chicken stock until smooth.

Return to heat and bring to the boil, stirring continuously, then remove from heat.

Place egg yolks in a small mixing bowl, add approximately ½ cup sauce, 2 tablespoons at a time, and beat well with a wire whisk. Gradually whisk in the cream.

Slowly whisk egg yolk-cream mixture into the sauce until smooth and creamy. Return saucepan to heat, bring slowly to the boil and simmer for 10 seconds. Season with salt, pepper and lemon juice.

Country Pancakes
Serves 6

12 pancakes
Filling:
250 g (8 oz) mushrooms, chopped
4 tomatoes, peeled and chopped
60 g (2 tablespoons) butter or margarine
300 ml (approx 1¼ cups) Cheese Sauce
1 small carton natural yoghurt
60 g (½ cup) grated Cheddar cheese
sprigs of fresh herbs for garnish

Prepare pancakes as directed in Basic Pancakes recipe (page 13) and keep hot.

Filling: Gently fry mushrooms and tomatoes in heated butter until reduced to a thick mixture.

To finish: Divide filling between pancakes, spread in a line over the bottom of each and roll up into cigar shapes.

Arrange stuffed pancakes in a buttered, ovenproof serving dish. Mix Cheese Sauce with yoghurt until smooth, then pour over the pancakes. Sprinkle with grated cheese and place under a medium-hot grill until bubbling hot.

Serve immediately garnished with fresh herbs.

Cheese Sauce
Makes 300 ml (approx 1¼ cups)

30 g (1 tablespoon) soft butter or polyunsaturated margarine
30 g (2 tablespoons) plain or all-purpose flour
300 ml (approx 1¼ cups) milk
pinch of mustard powder
salt
white pepper
60 g (½ cup) grated Cheddar cheese

Place soft butter, flour and milk all together in a heavy saucepan. Place over a medium heat and whisk continuously with a balloon-shaped wire whisk until the sauce boils.

Reduce heat to low and simmer for 1 minute. Stir in mustard powder and salt and pepper to taste, then add grated cheese and stir over the heat until cheese has dissolved.

If not ready to use sauce immediately, cover with a circle of wet greaseproof paper to prevent a skin forming.

Use to coat or fill crêpes according to directions in chosen recipe.

Cheese Pancakes with Cabbage

Serves 6

---

12 wholemeal pancakes
Filling:
45 g (1½ tablespoons) butter or margarine
500 g (4 cups) cabbage, finely shredded
1 large onion, finely chopped
60 g (⅓ cup) stoned raisins
½ teaspoon dill seeds
salt and pepper
½ teaspoon sugar
2 teaspoons tarragon vinegar
Cheese sauce:
30 g (1 tablespoon) butter or margarine
2 small onions, finely chopped
30 g (2 tablespoons) plain or all-purpose flour
300 ml (approx 1¼ cups) milk
60 g (¼ cup) Cheddar cheese, grated
½ teaspoon mustard powder
salt and pepper

Make pancakes as directed for Wholemeal Pancakes (page 17).

Filling: Melt half the butter or margarine in a large pan, add cabbage, cover and cook for 15 minutes. Lift out the cabbage with an egg slice or slotted spoon.

Add remaining butter to pan and fry onion, raisins and dill seeds for 5 minutes, or until onion is soft and transparent. Return cabbage to pan, season with salt and pepper and stir in the sugar and vinegar. Cover with a piece of buttered greaseproof paper, then cover with lid and simmer for 15 minutes.

Cheese sauce: Melt butter or margarine in a saucepan, add onions and fry until soft but not browned. Stir in the flour and remove from heat. Slowly add milk, stirring well. Return to heat and bring to the boil, stirring continuously, then reduce heat and simmer for 2 minutes. Remove from heat and stir in grated cheese, mustard, salt and pepper to taste.

To finish: Layer pancakes with hot filling on an ovenproof serving dish, ending with a pancake on top. Pour some of the cheese sauce over the top and keep the rest hot for serving at the table. Heat layered pancakes under a low grill or in a low oven until golden brown on top.

Cut pancakes into wedges and serve hot with remaining cheese sauce, accompanied with a tomato salad to add colour and variation in texture. Great for budgeters!

Ham and Mushroom Pancakes
Serves 6

12 pancakes
Filling:
75 g (2½ tablespoons) butter
1 onion, finely chopped
250 g (8 oz) mushrooms, finely chopped
1 teaspoon plain or all-purpose flour
4 tablespoons stock or cream
salt and pepper
1 tablespoon fresh chopped parsley and thyme
12 thin slices cooked ham
2 tablespoons grated Parmesan cheese

Prepare pancakes as directed for Basic Pancakes (page 13).

Filling: Melt 45 g (1½ tablespoons) butter in a frying pan and gently fry onion until soft but not browned. Add mushrooms and continue frying until all the moisture has evaporated.

Stir in the flour, then the stock or cream, salt and pepper and bring to the boil, stirring continuously. Add herbs and remove from heat.

To finish: Place a slice of ham on each pancake and top with a tablespoon of filling. Fold each pancake into quarters and place in a buttered, ovenproof dish. Melt remaining butter and brush over the pancakes.

Sprinkle with Parmesan cheese and bake in a hot oven at 200°C (400°F) for 7–10 minutes.

Serve hot with rings of hot, grilled pineapple.

Kidney Pancakes
Serves 6

12 pancakes
Filling:
3 lambs' kidneys
6 rashers bacon
1 onion, thinly sliced
15 g (1 tablespoon) plain or all-purpose flour
300 ml (approx 1¼ cups) beef stock, or use a stock cube
½ teaspoon dried thyme
salt and pepper
1 teaspoon tomato paste
1 tablespoon dry sherry, optional
chopped parsley for garnish

Cook pancakes as directed in Basic Pancakes recipe (page 13) and keep hot.

Filling: Skin kidneys, cut in half lengthways and, using scissors, remove core. Slice thinly. Remove rind and excess fat from bacon. Chop 4 rashers into small pieces.

Heat a frying pan, add bacon pieces and brown quickly. Remove bacon, add a little oil to the pan and quickly fry the sliced kidneys then remove from pan.

Fry onion until golden, stir in flour and cook for 2 minutes, stirring continuously. Remove from heat, add stock, thyme, salt and pepper, tomato paste and stir in well. Return to heat and bring to the boil, stirring continuously. Add bacon, kidneys and sherry, if used, cover and simmer for 15 minutes, then remove lid and allow liquid to reduce and thicken for 5 minutes.

Cut remaining rashers of bacon into short lengths, roll up tightly, thread on to a skewer and grill until cooked.

To finish: Spread hot filling on to hot pancakes, fold into quarters and arrange in a hot serving dish.

Serve piping hot with bacon rolls and sprinkled with chopped parsley, accompanied with halves of grilled tomatoes.

Potato Carrot Pancakes

Makes 20–24, serves 6–8

500 g (1 lb) potatoes
250 g (8 oz) carrots
1½ teaspoons salt
45 g (3 tablespoons) self-raising flour
¼ teaspoon white pepper
pinch of baking powder
2 eggs, beaten
margarine, lard or suet for greasing
sour cream for serving

Peel potatoes and carrots, cut potatoes into chunky pieces and slice carrots. Place in a pan with salt and 2.5 cm (1 inch) water, cover and bring to the boil, then simmer for 20 minutes until tender, drain well. Mash vegetables together until smooth, then stir in the flour, pepper, baking powder and beaten eggs.

Grease a griddle or heavy-based frying pan and place over a medium heat. Shape rounded metal tablespoonsful of mixture into neat rounds on the griddle. Fry until golden underneath, about 2 minutes, then turn over with a palette knife and cook other side until golden. Transfer pancakes to a warm plate and keep hot until all mixture is cooked.

Serve hot, with a bowl of sour cream to spoon on top, as a snack or as an accompaniment to frankfurters, sausages or barbecued lamb chops.

Sausage and Sauerkraut Pancakes

Serves 4–8 depending on appetite

8 pancakes
Filling:
1 × 440 g (14 oz) can sauerkraut
30 g (1 tablespoon) lard or oil
1 onion, finely chopped
2 tablespoons sour cream
4 thick bratwurst sausages
Sauce:
300 ml (1 carton) sour cream (use 2 tablespoons for filling)
2 teaspoons horseradish relish
2 teaspoons German mustard
pinch of salt

Prepare pancakes as for Basic Pancakes (page 13) and keep hot.

Filling: Drain sauerkraut, rinse in cold water and drain well again. Place sauerkraut in a pan, cover with freshly drawn, cold water and bring to the boil, then simmer, covered, for 5 minutes. Drain well.

Heat lard in a heavy pan and gently fry onion for 5 minutes. Stir in the sauerkraut and cook gently, stirring occasionally, for 10 minutes. Remove from heat, stir in 2 tablespoons sour cream and keep warm.

Meanwhile, bake or gently fry the bratwurst for 20 minutes or until cooked. Drain off fat, cut bratwurst in half lengthways and keep hot.

Sauce: Mix all ingredients together and place in a serving bowl or sauce boat.

To finish: Divide hot sauerkraut mixture between the pancakes, spread over centre and top each with half a bratwurst. Fold pancakes over and serve immediately while still hot accompanied with the sour cream sauce.

Savoury Herb Pancakes
Serves 6

12 pancakes
Filling:
185 g (¾ cup) mixed cooked chicken and ham, finely chopped
2 teaspoons dried mixed herbs
salt and pepper
30 g (1 tablespoon) butter or margarine
30 g (2 tablespoons) plain or all-purpose flour
300 ml (1¼ cups) chicken stock, or use a stock cube
1 tablespoon dry sherry, optional
2 tomatoes for garnish
30 g (2 tablespoons) toasted slivered almonds for garnish

Prepare pancakes according to Basic Pancakes recipe (page 13) and keep hot.

Filling: Mix together chicken, ham and herbs and season to taste with salt and pepper.

Melt butter in a saucepan, add flour, remove from heat and mix well. Stir in the stock gradually, to prevent lumps forming. Return to heat and bring to the boil, stirring continuously. Add sherry, if used.

Add sufficient sauce to chicken mixture to give it a spreading consistency.

To finish: Spread each pancake with hot filling, roll up and arrange in an ovenproof serving dish. Place in a hot oven at 200ºC (400ºF) for 10 minutes.

Serve hot garnished with lightly fried tomato segments and sprinkled with slivered almonds.

Savoury Layered Pancakes
Serves 6

12 wholemeal pancakes
Fillings:
1. 125 g (½ cup) chopped, cooked chicken
1 hard-boiled egg, chopped
2 tablespoons left-over gravy or cream

2. 30 g (1 tablespoon) butter or margarine
1 small onion or 4 shallots, chopped
4 tomatoes, chopped
1 tablespoon tomato sauce

3. 500 g (1 lb) silverbeet or spinach
30 g (1 tablespoon) butter or margarine
¼ teaspoon ground nutmeg

500 ml (2 cups) white sauce for coating
60 g (¼ cup) cheese, grated
salt and pepper
extra grated cheese for sprinkling

Prepare pancakes as directed in Wholemeal Pancakes recipe (page 17).

Fillings: 1. Mix chopped cooked chicken with chopped egg and gravy or cream.
2. Heat butter and fry onion until soft and golden. Add tomatoes and tomato sauce and simmer for 3–4 minutes.
3. Cook silverbeet in a small quantity of boiling salted water, drain well. Mix cooked silverbeet with butter and nutmeg.

To finish: Stack pancakes in layers on an ovenproof serving dish or baking dish, sandwiched together with alternate layers of the three savoury fillings.

Make white sauce and stir in the grated cheese and season to taste with salt and pepper. Pour sauce over pancakes, sprinkle grated cheese over top and place in a hot oven at 200°C (400°F) for 20–30 minutes or until piping hot. Cut in wedges and serve at once.

Turkey Crêpes
Serves 6

12 crêpes/pancakes
Filling:
2 cups diced cooked turkey
1 cup turkey stuffing
250 ml (1 cup) turkey gravy or rich stock
1 egg, beaten
cream to bind
salt and pepper
cranberry sauce for serving

Prepare crêpes as for French Crêpes recipe or pancakes as for Basic Pancakes recipe (page 13).

Filling: Mix turkey, turkey stuffing and gravy or stock together in a bowl with a fork. Add beaten egg and mix well. Stir in sufficient cream to bind mixture together. Season to taste with salt and pepper.

To finish: Divide filling between crêpes and spread across centre. Roll up crêpes and place in a buttered, shallow baking dish. Bake in a moderate oven at 180°C (350°F) for 20 minutes or until hot.

Serve immediately accompanied with cranberry sauce.

Note: A tasty dish which uses up left-over roast turkey.

Veal and Mushroom Crêpes

Serves 8 as a first course, 4 as a main course

8 crêpes/pancakes
Filling:
60 g (2 tablespoons) butter or margarine
1 small onion, chopped
125 g (4 oz) button mushrooms, sliced
250 g (8 oz) minced veal
2 tablespoons cream
1 tablespoon tomato paste
salt
white pepper
pinch of paprika
sour cream for serving

Prepare crêpes according to French Crêpes recipe or make pancakes according to Basic Pancakes recipe (page 13).

Filling: Melt butter in a small frying pan and gently fry onion and mushrooms for 3 minutes. Add the veal and stir with a fork so that it is well distributed.

Allow meat to brown slightly then add the cream, tomato paste and seasonings. Cook the mixture gently for 5–10 minutes to allow some of the liquid to evaporate.

To finish: Place approximately 2 tablespoons of filling in the centre of each crêpe and roll up.

Place crêpes in a greased ovenproof dish and heat through in a moderate oven at 180ºC (350ºF) for 15 minutes.

Serve immediately, topping each crêpe with some sour cream.

Wholemeal Spinach Pancakes with Tomato Sauce

Serves 6

12 wholemeal pancakes
Filling:
2 × 405 g (13 oz) cans spinach
30 g (1 tablespoon) butter or polyunsaturated margarine
1 tablespoon thinly sliced shallots
2 tablespoons cream
2 teaspoons tomato paste
½ teaspoon ground nutmeg
salt
freshly ground black pepper
Tomato Sauce for serving (page 52)

Prepare pancakes as in Wholemeal Pancakes recipe (page 17).

Filling: Drain spinach well in a sieve, pressing down with a wooden spoon, then place in a mixing bowl.

Heat butter or margarine in a small frying pan and gently fry shallots until soft but not browned. Drain shallots in a slotted spoon, then add to spinach. Add cream, tomato paste, nutmeg and salt and pepper to taste and mix together.

To finish: Place 2 tablespoons filling on each wholemeal pancake, spread over the centre and roll up in a cigar shape. Put pancakes in a buttered ovenproof baking dish or stack in layers on a round ovenproof plate, (see photograph).

Place pancakes in a hot oven at 200°C (400°F) for 15 minutes or until piping hot. Pour hot Tomato Sauce over and serve immediately.

Note: A 1 kg (2 lb) bunch of fresh spinach or silverbeet may be used in place of the canned spinach.

Tomato Sauce

Serves 6

15 g (2 teaspoons) dripping or oil
1 rasher bacon, rinded and finely chopped
1 onion, finely chopped
1 × 425 g (14 oz) can tomatoes or 500 g (1 lb) ripe tomatoes, peeled and chopped
4 tablespoons water or chicken stock
1 bay leaf
pinch of dried thyme
1 teaspoon salt
freshly ground black pepper
1 teaspoon arrowroot or cornflour blended with 1 tablespoon water

Heat dripping or oil in a heavy saucepan and gently fry bacon and onion for 5 minutes or until onion is soft and transparent.

Add tomatoes, water, bay leaf, thyme, salt and pepper and bring to the boil. Cover and simmer for 15 minutes.

Remove bay leaf, add blended arrowroot and bring back to boiling point, stirring continuously.

Serve sauce hot with Wholemeal Spinach Pancakes (page 51).

Crêpes
from Around
the World

Over the years, various nationalities throughout the world have developed their own version of the crêpe to suit their cuisine. Each country has given it a different name.

It is called a crêpe (rhymes with 'rep') in France, though Anglophiles pronounce it to rhyme with 'drape'.

In England, it is known as the homely pancake. It is always served there on Pancake Day or Shrove Tuesday, which is the last Tuesday before Lent and was originally a day of feasting to use up all the eggs, milk and butter in the household before the dietary restrictions of Lent began. Pancake races are still held in many places on Pancake Day, during which the competitors must toss their pancakes continuously from their pan while running the course.

In China, we find the egg roll/spring roll, the blini in Russia and Finland, the palacsinta in Hungary, krep in Greece, manicotti in Italy, the breakfast griddle cake in America and the corn tortilla in Mexico. Each of these is made from a different batter.

It's fun to experiment with crêpes from around the world. I hope you will discover an ethnic favourite among the following international recipes.

Acapulco Enchiladas

Serves 6

1 × 46 g (2 oz) packet enchilada sauce mix
1 × 185 g (6 oz) can tomato paste
750 ml (3 cups) cold water
2 cups diced cooked chicken
½ cup chopped olives
60 g (½ cup) slivered almonds
12 corn tortillas
oil, lard or white shortening for frying
125 g (1 cup) Cheddar cheese, grated
300 ml (1 carton) sour cream and
3 tablespoons thinly sliced shallots for serving

Place the enchilada sauce mix in a saucepan, add tomato paste and water and blend well. Bring mixture to the boil, stirring continuously, then reduce heat and simmer, without a lid, for 15 minutes, stirring occasionally.

Mix chicken, olives and almonds in a bowl with sufficient enchilada sauce to moisten, approximately ⅓ cup. Pour remaining sauce into a frying pan and keep hot.

Heat a shallow layer of oil in a frying pan and fry the tortillas, one by one, over a medium heat for a few seconds, just until they start to blister and turn limp.

Lift out each tortilla, using tongs, and dip it immediately into the sauce. Place the dipped tortilla on a board and spread one-twelfth of the chicken mixture over the centre. Roll up the tortilla and place it, sealed side down, in a shallow baking dish.

Continue in this way until all tortillas are filled.

Pour the remaining sauce over and sprinkle with grated cheese. Bake in a moderate oven at 180°C (350°F) for 15–20 minutes or until heated through.

Serve hot accompanied with sour cream mixed with shallots.

Note: Corn tortillas may be bought from specialty sections at some supermarkets or from the chef at certain Mexican restaurants. Alternatively, ask him where you can buy them.

Beef and Bean Enchiladas
Serves 6

---

500 g (1 lb) finely minced beef
1 onion, chopped
1 × 500 g (1 lb) can refried or baked beans
1 clove garlic, crushed
1 teaspoon salt
½ packet taco seasoning mix
125 ml (½ cup) water
1 packet enchilada sauce mix
6 tablespoons tomato paste
750 ml (3 cups) water
12 corn tortillas
oil for frying
250 g (8 oz) Cheddar cheese, grated
300 ml (1 carton) sour cream
sliced stuffed olives for garnish

Fry minced beef and onion in a heavy-based pan until all meat is browned, stirring frequently. Add beans, garlic, salt, taco seasoning mix and 125 ml water and bring to the boil, stirring frequently.

Blend enchilada sauce mix with tomato paste and a little of the remaining 750 ml water in a saucepan. Add remaining water and bring to the boil, stirring occasionally. Simmer for 10–15 minutes.

Heat 1 cm (½ inch) oil in a large, heavy frying pan and dip corn tortillas in, one at a time, turning over once as soon as they bubble up. Do not allow them to become crisp. Drain on absorbent kitchen paper towels.

Pour 1 cup enchilada sauce into the bottom of a shallow baking dish. Dip hot corn tortillas into hot enchilada sauce, one by one, to soften, then place ⅓ cup beef and bean filling on each and roll up to enclose filling. Place enchiladas, flap side down, in the dish of sauce. Pour remaining enchilada sauce over top. Sprinkle grated cheese over.

Bake in a moderate oven at 180⁰C (350⁰F) for 15–20 minutes or until heated through.

Serve hot with sour cream spooned over the top, garnished with sliced stuffed olives and accompanied with a bowl of preserved hot chillies.

Note: Enchiladas may be prepared in advance as far as heating in the oven. Store overnight in refrigerator then bake for 45 minutes before serving.

Chicken and Pepper Enchiladas

Serves 6

Filling:
2 chicken breasts
250 ml (1 cup) chicken stock
185 g (6 oz) packaged cream cheese
500 ml (2 cups) cream
1 onion, finely chopped
Sauce:
6 green banana peppers
500 g (1 lb) green tomatoes, skinned, seeded and chopped
2 green chillis, seeded and chopped
1 teaspoon ground coriander
1 egg
1 teaspoon salt
¼ teaspoon pepper
2 tablespoons lard for frying
12 tortillas
2 tablespoons grated Parmesan cheese

Filling: Place chicken in a heavy pan, add stock and simmer, covered, for 20 minutes or until tender. Transfer chicken to a plate to cool. Reserve stock. Shred chicken when cold.

Place cream cheese in a mixing bowl and beat in 6 tablespoons cream in two parts. Add onion and chicken and mix together.

Sauce: Place green peppers under a red-hot grill for 5 minutes, turning frequently, until they change colour but do not burn. Wrap peppers in a clean, damp tea towel and leave a few minutes, then remove cloth and gently rub peppers to remove all the skin.

Cut peppers in half and remove stalks, seeds and white membrane. Chop coarsely then mix to a purée in a blender or a food processor. Add tomatoes, green chilli, coriander and 3 tablespoons reserved chicken stock and mix to a smooth purée.

Add remaining cream, egg, salt and pepper and mix again until smooth. Pour sauce into a frying pan.

To finish: Heat lard in a frying pan on a medium heat and fry tortillas, one by one, for a few seconds on both sides until they blister. Drain tortillas and immediately dip into pan of hot sauce until limp. Transfer tortillas to a plate, spread 3 tablespoons filling along centre and roll up.

Place filled enchiladas, sealed side down, in a large, shallow baking dish. Pour remaining sauce over, sprinkle with Parmesan cheese and bake in a moderate oven at 180°C (350°F) for 15 minutes or until hot and golden.

Serve immediately.

Blini
Serves 6-8, 2 blini per person

Batter:
1 × 7 g (¼ oz) packet dry yeast or 15 g (1 oz) fresh yeast
¼ cup lukewarm water
250 g (2 cups) buckwheat flour or wholemeal flour or mixture of both
½ teaspoon salt
125 ml (½ cup) lukewarm cream
1 egg, beaten
60 g (2 tablespoons) melted butter
250 ml (1 cup) boiling milk
2 tablespoons vodka, optional
unsalted butter for frying
For serving:
125 g (½ cup) melted butter
60 g (2 oz) red caviar
60 g (2 oz) black caviar
2 pickled herrings
125 g (4 oz) smoked salmon
300 ml (1 carton) sour cream
½ bunch thinly sliced shallots

Batter: Dissolve yeast in lukewarm water. Place flour into a warm mixing bowl, add salt and make a well in the centre. Pour yeast into centre of flour, add lukewarm cream and stir in flour from edge of bowl with a wooden spoon. Add beaten egg and melted butter and beat until batter is smooth.

Cover bowl with clear plastic wrap, then wrap securely in a thick towel and stand it in a warm place to rise for 4 hours, then stir boiling milk into the yeast batter until smooth.

To cook blini: Brush the bottom of an 18 cm (7 inch) crêpe pan with melted unsalted butter. Heat pan over a medium-high heat and pour in a large cooking spoonful of batter (equal to 3 measuring tablespoons of batter). Cook blini over a medium-high heat, moving pan occasionally to prevent sticking. When blini is golden brown underneath, loosen very carefully with a palette knife and turn over and cook other side until golden. Slide blini out on to a warm serving plate and serve immediately or keep hot in a warm oven while cooking rest of batter.

Serve sprinkled with melted butter, then topped with either red or black caviar, pickled herrings or smoked salmon, then top with sour cream and sliced shallots. The guests help themselves to the toppings. Blini are eaten with a knife and fork.

Ham Strudel with Mushroom Sauce

Serves 8-12

---

500 g (1 lb) cooked lean ham
2 egg yolks
2 tablespoons sour cream
freshly ground black pepper
16 pancakes (page 13)
2 white linen serviettes
white string
60 g (½ cup) freshly grated Parmesan cheese
chopped chives or parsley for garnish
Mushroom Sauce (page 61)

Trim all fat and tissues off ham and mince ham finely. Place in a mixing bowl and stir in egg yolks, sour cream and pepper to taste.

Arrange 8 pancakes, overlapping approximately 2.5 cm (1 inch), in a long row on a clean, white, linen serviette (damask is best but clean fine tea towels may be substituted).

Place half ham mixture along centre of pancakes. Fold in short sides of pancakes and roll up neatly from one long side to the other.

Carefully transfer pancake roll to the lower edge of the serviette, then roll up serviette from bottom edge to top to form a long roll, enclosing the pancake roll. Tie neatly with white string, folding in ends securely.

Fill the remaining pancakes in the same way and wrap them securely in the second serviette.

Bring a large pan of water to boiling point, lower both rolls in gently, bending into a horseshoe shape, and boil rapidly for 10 minutes.

To serve, remove from pan, cut string, unroll serviette, place 'strudel' on a long, warm serving plate and sprinkle with Parmesan cheese and chopped chives. Serve immediately, cut in thick oblique slices, accompanied with Mushroom Sauce.

Note: This unusual but delicious recipe, attributed to a Hungarian farmer's wife, has been handed down over the years.

Mushroom Sauce
Serves 8

30 g (1 tablespoon) butter, margarine, or
white shortening
750 g (1½ lb) button mushrooms, sliced
15 g (1 tablespoon) plain or all-purpose flour
300 ml (1 carton) sour cream (minus 2 tablespoons for
filling for Ham Strudel, page 60)
3 tablespoons water

Heat butter in a heavy saucepan, add mushrooms and gently fry until all liquid has evaporated. Cool, transfer to a covered container, then chill in refrigerator overnight or for 1–2 days to give mushrooms a good black colour.

Return mushrooms to saucepan, heat gently and sprinkle flour over. Stir over a medium heat for 1 minute. Add sour cream and water and bring to the boil, stirring continuously.

Serve sauce hot in a warm sauceboat as an accompaniment to Ham Strudel.

Note: The chilling process may be omitted but the sauce will have a lighter colour.

German Potato Pancakes
Serves 6-8

6 medium-sized potatoes (approx 1 kg/2 lb)
45 g (3 tablespoons) plain or all-purpose flour
1 teaspoon salt
2 eggs, beaten
1 tablespoon finely grated onion
125 g (4 tablespoons) lard

Peel potatoes and place in a bowl of cold water. Pat dry and grate coarsely then drain well in a colander or sieve, pressing down well to squeeze out as much moisture as possible.

Sift flour and salt into a mixing bowl. Add beaten egg gradually and beat with a wooden spoon until smooth. Stir in grated onion and potato.

Heat lard on a griddle or in a heavy frying pan and pour on 4 metal tablespoons of batter. Shape in to a pancake 12 cm (5 inches) in diameter, using a palette knife or fish slice, and fry over a medium heat until golden brown and set, turn and fry other side until golden. Remove from pan and keep warm in a low oven. Continue making pancakes in this way with rest of potato batter.

Serve hot with goulash or a casserole in place of boiled potatoes.

Lasagne with Pancakes
Serves 6

12 pancakes
1 onion, chopped
2 cloves garlic, crushed
2 tablespoons olive oil
500 g (1 lb) finely minced topside
250 ml (1 cup) water
1 beef stock cube
grated rind of 1 lemon
1 bay leaf
1 × 185 g (6 oz) can tomato paste
1 teaspoon salt
freshly ground black pepper
125 ml (½ cup) red wine
250 g (8 oz) ricotta or cottage cheese
1 egg, beaten
2 tablespoons chopped parsley
250 g (8 oz) mozzarella cheese

Prepare pancakes according to Basic Pancakes recipe (page 13).

Gently fry onion and garlic in olive oil in a large, heavy-based pan for 3–5 minutes. Add minced topside and stir over heat until browned. Add water, crumbled stock cube, lemon rind, bay leaf, tomato paste, salt, pepper and wine. Bring to the boil, stirring occasionally, then reduce heat and simmer, covered, for 30 minutes.

Place a layer of meat sauce in a large, shallow, greased baking dish, then cover with a layer of pancakes. Mix ricotta or cottage cheese with beaten egg and parsley and place a layer of mixture over the pancakes. Cover with another layer of pancakes.

Repeat layers, finishing with a layer of meat sauce. Cover with thin slices of mozzarella cheese. Bake in a moderate oven at 180⁰C (350⁰F) for 30–40 minutes or until cheese topping has melted and sauce is bubbling hot.

Serve immediately, followed by a tossed salad.

Manicotta Pancakes

Serves 6

12 pancakes
Filling:
1 onion, chopped
1 clove garlic, crushed
30 g (1 tablespoon) butter or olive oil
500 g (1 lb) finely minced beef
1 × 405 g (13 oz) can spinach, drained
125 g (½ cup) cottage cheese
2 tablespoons grated Parmesan cheese
1 teaspoon salt
¼ teaspoon pepper
Sauce:
60 g (2 tablespoons) butter
60 g (4 tablespoons) plain or all-purpose flour
625 ml (2½ cups) milk
3 tablespoons grated Parmesan cheese
salt and pepper

Make pancakes according to Basic Pancakes recipe (page 13).

Filling: Gently fry onion and garlic in heated butter in a large frying pan. Add beef and stir until browned. Remove from heat and drain off excess fat. Add spinach, cheeses, salt and pepper and mix well.

Divide filling between pancakes and roll up. Place in a large, shallow, buttered baking dish.

Sauce: Melt butter in a saucepan, stir in flour over a medium heat for 1 minute. Add milk gradually and bring to the boil, stirring continuously. Stir in Parmesan cheese and salt and pepper to taste.

To finish: Pour sauce over pancakes and cook in a moderate oven at 180°C (350°F) for 20–30 minutes, until meat is tender and sauce is bubbling hot.

Paprika Chicken with Pancakes

Serves 6

90 g (3 tablespoons) lard or white shortening
2 onions, finely chopped
2 teaspoons paprika pepper
1 × 3 kg (1½ lb) dressed chicken
1 chicken breast (schnitzel)
salt
1 green pepper, seeded and chopped
1 large tomato, chopped
300 ml (1 carton) sour cream
14 pancakes (page 13)

Heat lard in a heavy-based pan and gently fry onion until soft and transparent but not brown. Push onion to side of pan, remove from heat and stir paprika into remaining lard and juices.

Joint chicken, discard backbone and remove skin from breast and legs. Cut chicken breast in half. Sprinkle chicken pieces with salt.

Return pan to heat, add chicken pieces and stir for 4–5 minutes, until chicken has changed colour all over. Cover and simmer on a very low heat for 15–20 minutes.

Add green pepper and tomato and simmer, covered, for a further 15–20 minutes, until chicken is tender, then allow to cool.

Transfer chicken pieces to a board, remove chicken meat from bones and cut chicken into 2.5 cm (1 inch) pieces. Return chicken to juices in pan, add sour cream and stir all together.

Roll up 6 stacked pancakes to form a cigar-shaped roll and cut into 1 cm (½ inch) slices. Repeat with a further 6 pancakes. Gently stir sliced pancakes into paprika chicken mixture.

Place mixture in a large, greased baking dish or casserole and cover top with the 2 remaining pancakes. Place in a cold oven, then set temperature at 200⁰C (400⁰F) and heat through for ¾–1 hour or until bubbling hot.

Remove pancake 'lid' and serve hot as a main course, followed by a tossed salad.

Paprika Chicken with Pancakes

Overleaf, left: Swiss Pancakes

Overleaf, right: Apple Pancakes Longueville

Won Tons

Serves 8–10

---

40 won ton wrappers
Filling:
1 cup shredded green cabbage
1 stalk celery, thinly sliced
125 g (4 oz) cooked prawns or shrimps
125 g (4 oz) cooked chicken livers
125 g (4 oz) roast pork
5 water chestnuts, finely chopped
¼ cup julienne strips of bamboo shoots
beaten egg for glaze
oil for deep frying
Sweet and Sour Sauce for serving (page 71)

Won ton wrappers are small squares of pressed dough available in Chinese food stores. Store in refrigerator until required.

Filling: Place cabbage and celery in a pan with a small amount of water and boil for 5 minutes. Drain well and shred vegetables finely.

Chop prawns, chicken livers and roast pork finely and mix with shredded vegetables. Add water chestnuts and bamboo shoots and mix well.

To finish: Place a rounded teaspoon of filling in centre of the dull side of every won ton wrapper. (Shape approximately 5 at a time.) Brush edges of won ton wrappers with beaten egg, fold bottom corner up and over filling, shaping the filling into a cylinder. Fold left and right corners of wrapper over like an envelope, then roll won ton up securely, enclosing filling. Continue until all filling is used.

Deep fry won tons, approximately 6–8 at a time, in oil in a wok at 175°C (350°F) until crisp and golden, about 5 minutes. Drain well and keep hot, until all the won tons are cooked.

Serve won tons coated with hot Sweet and Sour Sauce. Eat with chopsticks.

Spring Rolls and Won Tons with Sweet and Sour Sauce

Spring Rolls
Makes 12

---

12 spring roll pancakes or shells
Pork and shrimp filling:
185 g (6 oz) pork fillet
3 tablespoons oil
1 × 185 g (6 oz) can shrimps
6 water chestnuts, finely chopped
8 shallots, thinly sliced
1 tablespoon soy sauce
1 teaspoon salt
or
Chicken filling:
1 chicken breast
1 teaspoon cornflour (cornstarch)
½ teaspoon salt
½ teaspoon sugar
2 tablespoons soy sauce
2 tablespoons oil
3 shallots, thinly sliced
¼ cup bamboo shoots, finely chopped
1½ cups bean sprouts

Prepare pancakes according to Spring Roll Pancakes recipe (page 16).

Pork and shrimp filling: Trim all fat and tissue from pork and cut meat into julienne strips, 5 × 25 mm (¼ × 1 inch).

Heat oil in a small frying pan and fry pork for 5 minutes, stirring frequently with a wooden spoon.

Drain and rinse shrimps in cold water. Add shrimps, water chestnuts and shallots to pork and cook for 5 minutes. Stir in soy sauce and salt, remove from heat and allow to cool.

Chicken filling: Cut chicken into julienne strips, place in a small bowl and mix with cornflour, salt, sugar and 1 tablespoon soy sauce. Allow to marinate for 10 minutes.

Heat 1 tablespoon oil in a small frying pan and gently fry vegetable ingredients for 2–3 minutes. Stir in remaining soy sauce and remove from pan.

Heat remaining oil in frying pan and fry chicken mixture for 2–3 minutes. Stir vegetable mixture into chicken mixture and simmer for a further 2 minutes then leave to cool.

To finish: Place 1 tablespoon of chosen filling in a line along the lower half of pancake. Brush edges of pancake with beaten egg (or some left-over pancake batter). Fold bottom of pancake over then fold sides in to make an envelope, roll up tightly and secure with 2 wooden toothpicks to keep in shape.

Heat oil in a deep frying pan, or an electric deep fryer, to 190°C (375°F) and deep fry rolls, 2 or 3 at a time, for 2 minutes or until crisp and golden brown. Drain well on absorbent kitchen paper.

Serve spring rolls hot with soy sauce, vinegar and mustard for dipping. The spring rolls may be eaten with either chopsticks or a knife and fork. For a buffet party, wrap a small paper napkin around each roll and eat it with your fingers.

Note: Spring roll shells may be bought from Chinese/Oriental food stores.

Sweet and Sour Sauce
Makes approx 625 ml (2½ cups)

1 teaspoon oil
½ teaspoon finely chopped root ginger
1 carrot, in julienne strips
2 slices pineapple, chopped
3 teaspoons cornflour (cornstarch)
1½ tablespoons sugar
1 tablespoon soy sauce
2 tablespoons vinegar
1 tablespoon dry sherry or brandy
375 ml (1½ cups) water
3 shallots, thinly sliced

Heat oil in a small pan and gently fry the ginger, carrot and pineapple for 2 minutes.

Blend the cornflour and sugar in a small mixing bowl with the soy sauce, vinegar and sherry until smooth. Add blended mixture to pan along with water and bring to the boil, stirring continuously. Add shallots and simmer for 3–4 minutes.

Serve with hot Won Tons.

Filipino Lumpia
Makes 12

12 lumpia, egg roll wrappers or spring roll shells
Filling:
1 kg (2 lb) chicken or chicken pieces
250 g (8 oz) lean pork shoulder
1 onion, quartered
green tops of 2 celery stalks
1 bay leaf
3 teaspoons salt
500 ml (2 cups) water
500 g (1 lb) green cabbage
500 g (1 lb) green beans
125 g (4 oz) bean sprouts
1 small onion, thinly sliced
2 teaspoons crushed garlic
½ cup finely chopped celery
125 g (4 oz) bacon, in a piece
2 tablespoons soy sauce
oil for deep frying
12 lettuce leaves for serving
fresh coriander leaves for garnish

Prepare lumpia according to directions for Pancakes for Spring Rolls recipe (page 16).

Filling: Cut chicken into 6 or 8 pieces. Cut pork into 4 chunky pieces. Place chicken, pork, onion, celery tops, bay leaf, 1 teaspoon salt and water into a heavy pan. Cover and bring to the boil, then reduce heat and simmer for 20–30 minutes or until meat is tender. Allow to cool, then remove chicken and pork. Skin and bone chicken and dice chicken meat and pork. Strain chicken stock and reserve ½ cup.

Wash and trim cabbage, cut into segments, remove white cores and shred cabbage finely, cutting crosswise. Wash, trim and string beans and cut diagonally into 5 mm (¼ inch) pieces. Wash bean sprouts in cold water, remove husks and drain well. Prepare onion, garlic, celery and chop bacon.

Place bacon in a heavy frying pan and fry in its own fat over medium heat until crisp, remove bacon and drain well. Place onion and garlic in pan and fry in bacon fat for 5 minutes, stirring frequently. Stir in chicken and pork and stir-fry for 1 or 2 minutes until meat browns. Add beans, bean sprouts, celery and cabbage a handful at a time, in given order, and stir-fry each for 1 or 2 minutes. Add bacon, reserved stock, soy sauce and 2 teaspoons salt and stir over medium heat for 3 minutes.

Transfer chicken and vegetable mixture to a colander standing in a mixing bowl and allow to drain for 10–15 minutes. Discard liquid.

To finish: Keep egg roll wrappers covered with a tea towel and make lumpia one at a time. Place ⅓ cup filling in a cylinder shape in the centre of an egg roll wrapper. Fold one corner over, fold each side corner over, then roll up tightly. Cover the lumpia with a tea towel as each one is filled.

Heat 3 cups oil in a wok or an electric deep fryer to 180°C (375°F). Place 3 or 4 lumpia in the hot oil, seam side down, and deep fry for 2 minutes or until crisp and golden. Drain well on kitchen paper.

Serve lumpia piping hot as soon as they are fried, wrapped in a lettuce leaf, and arranged in a pyramid, garnished with fresh coriander leaves.

Note: Egg roll wrappers, fresh bean sprouts and coriander leaves may be bought in leading Chinese stores.

Austrian Kaiserschmarrn
Serves 4–6

2 tablespoons seedless raisins
4 tablespoons dark rum
4 egg yolks
3 tablespoons sugar
pinch of salt
500 ml (2 cups) milk
1 teaspoon vanilla essence
125 g (1 cup) continental flour
5 egg whites
4 tablespoons unsalted butter, melted
icing sugar and fruit purée for serving

Soak raisins in rum for 30 minutes, then drain and squeeze dry.

Place egg yolks, sugar and salt in a mixing bowl and beat with an electric mixer or rotary beater until thick. Stir in the milk and vanilla essence, then gradually beat in the flour in two parts, beating well until smooth. Add the raisins.

Whisk egg whites until stiff and gently fold into basic mixture.

Heat 1 tablespoon melted butter in a 20 cm (8 inch) crêpe pan over a low heat, pour in half the batter and cook until slightly browned and puffed, about 4 minutes. Turn pancake over on to a plate, add another tablespoon melted butter to pan, heat through, then slide pancake back into pan and cook until golden underneath.

With 2 forks, tear the pancake into 8 pieces, then place on a warm plate and keep warm.

Cook the rest of the batter in the remaining butter, as described above, and pull into 8 pieces in the same way. Return the first pieces of pancake to the pan and heat through gently for 2 minutes, turning over occasionally.

Serve immediately, sprinkled generously with icing sugar and accompanied with warm apple, apricot or blackcurrant purée.

Continental flour is sold in leading delicatessens.

Crêpes Suzette
Serves 8

16 crêpes
Sauce:
6 cubes of sugar
2 large oranges
1 large lemon
125 g (½ cup) unsalted butter
30 g (1 tablespoon) caster sugar
3 tablespoons Grand Marnier
2 tablespoons dark rum

Prepare crêpes as given in French Crêpes recipe (page 13) but substitute 4 tablespoons Grand Marnier for the 4 tablespoons water. Make crêpes in a small crêpe pan, approximately 12 cm (5 inches) wide.

Sauce: Rub 3 cubes of sugar over the oranges until they are saturated with the oils of the rind. Rub the other 3 cubes of sugar over the lemon until soaked with the oil of the lemon rind.

Squeeze the juice from the oranges and measure 6 tablespoons juice into a small bowl. Add the sugar cubes to the juice and crush with a spoon until dissolved.

Soften the butter and cream with the sugar until light and smooth.

To finish: Place the creamed butter mixture in a flambé pan and stir over a spirit burner until melted. Add orange juice mixture and bring to the boil, stirring continuously.

Place a crêpe in the sauce, turn it over with a spoon and fork to moisten both sides, then fold into quarters. Push to side of pan and moisten and fold remaining crêpes as directed and arrange them in overlapping rows.

Pour Grand Marnier and rum into pan and light to flambé. Shake pan gently over burner until flames die, then spoon hot sauce over crêpes and serve immediately.

Dutch Apple Pancakes

*Makes 5-6 large pancakes, depending on
size of frying pan*

500 g (4 cups) plain or all-purpose flour
pinch of salt
30 g (1 oz) fresh yeast or 2 × 7 g (¼ oz) packets dry yeast
1 teaspoon sugar
1 litre (4 cups) lukewarm milk
4 small apples
lemon juice
250 g (1 cup) unsalted butter or polyunsaturated margarine for cooking
brown sugar
ground cinnamon
maple syrup for serving

Sift flour and salt into a large, warm mixing bowl. Make a well in the centre. Cream (mix) yeast with 1 teaspoon sugar in a small bowl. Pour yeast into centre of flour. Add 2 cups lukewarm milk to centre of flour and mix to a smooth batter with a wooden spoon. Stir in remaining milk.

Cover bowl and put batter in a warm place to rise for 45 minutes.

Meanwhile, peel, core and slice apples. Cover with cold water and a squeeze of lemon juice to prevent browning and put aside until required.

To cook pancakes, melt 30 g (1 tablespoon) butter in a large, heavy frying pan (choose a pan which is the same size as a dinner plate). Pour in ¾–1 cup of batter, put some sliced apple on top of the batter and fry the pancake until golden underneath. Turn pancake over using a palette knife and an egg slice and add another ½ tablespoon butter to the pan. Cook on other side until golden.

Slide pancake on to a hot dinner plate and serve immediately sprinkled with brown sugar and ground cinnamon and accompanied with maple syrup.

Make four or five more pancakes as described, allowing ¾–1 cup batter per pancake and approximately 45 g (1½ tablespoons) butter for frying each one.

Note: It is a good idea, when making these, to use two frying pans, so that you do not keep the family waiting too long. These are very satisfying on a cold, bleak, winter's day.

Greek Krep

Makes 20-24, serves 8-12

---

125 g (1 cup) plain or all-purpose flour
1 tablespoon ground cinnamon
1 tablespoon finely grated lemon rind
pinch of salt
2 large eggs
60 g (¼ cup) caster sugar
500 ml (2 cups) milk
1 tablespoon vanilla essence
oil for cooking
jam for serving

Sift flour and cinnamon into a mixing bowl and add the lemon rind and salt.

Beat eggs with sugar, then beat in the milk and vanilla essence.

Make a well in the centre of the dry ingredients and gradually beat in the liquids until smooth.

Cook pancakes in a small crêpe pan, as directed, until lightly browned on both sides and keep hot.

Spread each pancake or krep with jam, roll up tightly and serve immediately.

Irish Peach Pancakes

Makes 16, serves 8

Batter:
250 g (2 cups) plain or all-purpose flour
1 large egg
2 egg yolks
500 ml (2 cups) milk
Filling:
4 peaches
125 ml (½ cup) Irish whiskey
300 ml (1 carton) thickened cream
extra 2 tablespoons Irish whiskey

Batter: Sift flour into a large mixing bowl. Make a well in the centre, add egg and egg yolks and mix with a little flour. Gradually add half the milk and beat in the flour with a wooden spoon until smooth. Stir in remaining milk and beat well.

Cover batter and allow to stand while preparing filling.

Filling: Peel peaches, cut in half and remove stone. Dice peaches and place in a pan with 125 ml Irish whiskey. Heat gently then transfer to a bowl and leave to cool and macerate.

Make pancakes as directed for Cooking Crêpes (page 18), layering them on a heatproof plate with strips of greaseproof paper between them, until all batter is cooked. Cover with foil and heat pancakes either by placing in a moderate oven at 180°C (350°F) or by standing over a large pan half full of boiling water for 15 minutes or until hot.

Meanwhile, whip cream and fold in the extra Irish whiskey.

Serve hot pancakes open on individual plates topped with the peach filling and the whipped flavoured cream.

Swedish Pancake Gâteau
Serves 6-8

Pancakes:
185 g (1½ cups) plain or all-purpose flour
½ teaspoon salt
60 g (¼ cup) caster sugar
3 large eggs
375 ml (1½ cups) milk
4 tablespoons melted unsalted butter
oil for frying

Filling:
2 cups chunky apple sauce or canned pie apple
300 ml (1 carton) thickened cream
2 tablespoons icing sugar

Pancakes: Sift flour and salt into a mixing bowl and add sugar. Beat eggs and mix with milk and melted butter. Gradually add liquids to dry ingredients, beating well with a wooden spoon, until the batter is smooth.

Cook pancakes in oil, as directed, in a 20 cm (8 inch) crêpe pan, and stack on a flat plate.

To finish: Put a pancake on a flat serving plate and spread with a layer of apple sauce. Place alternate layers of pancakes and apple sauce on top of this, finishing with a pancake.

Whip cream until thick and fold in the icing sugar. Completely cover the layered gâteau with the whipped cream and chill in refrigerator.

Serve cut in wedges.

From Breakfast to Tea

Griddle cakes are a popular breakfast dish with millions of Americans and are spreading to other corners of the world. The basic griddle cake, called pancake in some states, is delicious served hot in a stack of four or five, topped with soft butter and drenched with maple syrup. If you don't fancy them for breakfast, try them for a delicious after-the-show supper. They are also good accompanied with fresh fruit salad and yoghurt for an extremely healthy breakfast.

I am giving you a few variations of the breakfast griddle cake. Try making the Light Breakfast Pancakes with fresh snow in place of water for a really light result.

Again, for those interested in good nutrition, try the Cornmeal Hot Cakes and the Swedish Oatmeal Pancakes hot from the pan.

When it comes to afternoon tea, it is very hard to by-pass delicious Scots Pancakes. I have happy childhood memories of eating these straight from the griddle, in my mother's kitchen, topped with butter and golden syrup or home-made blackberry jelly. A delicious variation of these is Swiss Pancakes, another afternoon tea treat.

American Pancakes with Maple Syrup

Makes 12-16, serves 3-4

250 g (2 cups) plain or all-purpose flour
2 teaspoons baking powder
2 teaspoons sugar
1 teaspoon salt
3 eggs, lightly beaten
500 ml (2 cups) milk
60 g (2 tablespoons) butter or polyunsaturated margarine, melted
4 tablespoons vegetable oil for cooking
whipped butter and maple syrup for serving

Sift flour, baking powder, sugar and salt into a large mixing bowl. Make a well in centre of flour and pour in beaten eggs and milk. Mix with a wooden spoon until smooth then stir in the melted butter. Do not overbeat.

Heat a griddle or small, heavy frying pan over a medium heat until a drop of water flicked on it evaporates quickly. Lightly brush griddle or pan with oil, using a pastry brush, and pour approximately ½ cup batter on to the hot pan to form an 8–10 cm (3–4 inch) diameter pancake. Cook for 2–3 minutes until small bubbles form on the surface. Turn over with a palette knife and cook for 1 minute on other side until golden brown.

Stack pancakes on a heated plate and serve hot with whipped butter and maple syrup for breakfast or brunch. Serve a stack of 3 or 4 pancakes per person.

Light Breakfast Pancakes

Makes approx 26 pancakes, serves 6-8

125 g (1 cup) plain or all-purpose flour
¼ teaspoon salt
2 eggs, separated
300 ml (approx 1¼ cups) water
200 ml (1 small jar) thickened cream
unsalted butter for cooking

Sift flour and salt into a mixing bowl. Beat egg yolks and water together. Make a well in centre of flour and add the beaten egg and water mixture. Gradually stir in the flour.

When batter is blended and smooth, whip the cream until thick and fold it into the batter. Whisk the egg whites to a stiff foam and gently fold into the batter.

Heat a griddle or an electric frying pan and melt about 2 teaspoons unsalted butter on/in it so that it is coated all over.

Pour approximately 2 tablespoons batter on to the griddle, from the tip of a metal cooking spoon, to form a small round. Repeat this process, shaping more pancakes, but allow space for spreading and turning pancakes. Cook on both sides until golden.

Serve hot, fresh from the griddle, with stewed cherries for breakfast.

Cornmeal Hot Cakes

Makes approx 30 hot cakes, serves approx 8

375 ml (1½ cups) water
220 g (1⅓ cups) cornmeal
435 ml (1¾ cups) milk
1 tablespoon molasses
60 g (2 tablespoons) melted butter
2 egg yolks, beaten
90 g (¾ cup) wholemeal flour, finely ground
1 teaspoon salt
1 teaspoon baking powder
2 egg whites
unsalted butter for cooking

Bring 375 ml water to the boil in a saucepan, then stir in the cornmeal. Remove from heat and allow to stand for 10 minutes.

Transfer cornmeal mixture to a large mixing bowl, add milk, molasses, butter and beaten egg yolks and mix together.

Into another bowl or on to a sheet of greaseproof paper, sift the wholemeal flour, salt and baking powder. Add these dry ingredients to the cornmeal mixture and beat well until mixture is well blended.

Whisk egg whites until stiff peaks form and gently fold into the mixture.

Heat a griddle or an electric frying pan and melt about 2 teaspoons of unsalted butter on/in it until coated all over.

Pour approximately 1½ tablespoons of batter into the pan from the tip of a metal cooking spoon, to form a small round. Repeat this process, allowing space between cakes for spreading and turning. Cook hot cakes on both sides until golden.

Serve hot from the pan with crisply fried bacon rashers or sausages for breakfast, or as a main course with grilled pork chops and apple rings.

Savoury Griddle Cakes
Serves 6

250 g (2 cups) plain or all-purpose flour
2 teaspoons baking powder
2 teaspoons sugar
1 teaspoon salt
¼ teaspoon pepper
3 eggs
500 ml (2 cups) milk
60 g (2 tablespoons) butter, melted
3 rashers bacon, chopped and fried
1 × 310 g (10 oz) can sweet corn kernels, drained
1 tablespoon chopped herbs
oil for cooking

Sift flour, baking powder, sugar, salt and pepper into a mixing bowl. Make a well in the centre and pour in the eggs and milk. Mix with a wooden spoon, then beat until smooth. Stir in melted butter, bacon, sweet corn and herbs.

Heat a griddle or a large, heavy frying pan over a medium heat until a drop of water flicked on to it evaporates quickly. Brush hot griddle with oil, then pour ½ cup savoury batter on to it to form an 8–10 cm (3–4 inch) pancake. Cook until small bubbles form on top of griddle cake, then turn over, using a palette knife, and cook until other side is golden brown. Keep hot until all mixture is cooked.

Serve griddle cakes immediately, topped with fried or scrambled eggs for breakfast.

Swedish Oatmeal Pancakes

Makes approx 24 pancakes, serves 8–12

185 g (2 cups) rolled oats
500 ml (2 cups) buttermilk
60 g (½ cup) plain or all-purpose flour
1½ tablespoons sugar
½ teaspoon baking powder
2 eggs, beaten
60 g (2 tablespoons) melted butter
extra 2 tablespoons buttermilk, if necessary
unsalted butter for cooking

In a large mixing bowl, mix together the rolled oats and 500 ml buttermilk with a wooden spoon, cover and refrigerate for at least 2 hours.

Sift flour, sugar and baking powder together on to a sheet of greaseproof paper. Add sifted dry ingredients to rolled oats mixture and beat until thoroughly combined. Add beaten eggs and melted butter and mix well. Stir in extra buttermilk if the mixture is too thick to pour.

Heat a griddle or a large heavy frying pan and add at least 2 teaspoons melted unsalted butter to the griddle before each addition of mixture.

Drop approximately 2 tablespoons of batter on to the griddle for each pancake and allow to form neat rounds. Cook the pancakes until the undersides are browned, turn over with a palette knife and cook the other side until browned. Place on a tea towel on a wire cooking tray and cover with another tea towel to keep warm while cooking the remaining batter.

Serve the pancakes hot with apple sauce or apricot conserve and sour cream for breakfast.

Scots Pancakes
(Drop Scones or Pikelets)
Makes approx 16

125 g (1 cup) self-raising flour *or*
125 g (1 cup) plain or all-purpose flour sifted with
¼ teaspoon bicarbonate of soda and
¼ teaspoon cream of tartar
30 g (1 tablespoon) caster sugar
1 large egg
150 ml buttermilk or milk
lard or suet for greasing

Sift flour and sugar into a mixing bowl. Make a well in the centre, add egg and buttermilk gradually and beat in with a wooden spoon until smooth.

Lightly grease a griddle (or heavy-based frying pan) with lard or rub with a piece of suet wrapped in muslin and place over a medium heat. When hot, drop one metal tablespoon of batter from the tip of the spoon on to the griddle to form a neat round. Continue until griddle is covered with pancakes but allow plenty of space around each one for turning over. When the surfaces begin to bubble and the undersides are slightly golden, turn pancakes over with a palette knife and cook other sides until golden and cooked in the centre.

Place on a clean tea towel on a wire cooling tray and cover with another tea towel until cool, unless they are to be eaten hot. Serve with butter and jam or honey and whipped cream while still warm, or serve cold.

Note: These may be cooked very successfully in an electric frying pan.

Scots pancakes must be eaten as fresh as possible the day they are made. Stale pancakes are good fried up with bacon and eggs for breakfast.

Swiss Pancakes

Makes 8

---

16 Scots Pancakes (page 88).
250 g (8 oz) packet cream cheese
2 teaspoons caster sugar
4 drops vanilla essence
300 ml (1 large jar) thickened cream
250 g (8 oz) black cherry jam

Prepare Scots Pancakes as directed.

Place cream cheese in a mixing bowl, add caster sugar, vanilla essence and 3 tablespoons cream and beat well until smooth.

Spread the cream cheese mixture over 8 pancakes and top with the remaining 8 pancakes.

Place the sandwiched pancakes on a grill pan and carefully put a teaspoon of cream on top of each one. Place under a very hot grill for $\frac{1}{2}$–1 minute.

Place 1 or 2 teaspoons black cherry jam on top of each Swiss pancake and serve immediately with a bowl of remaining cream, whipped, and extra black cherry jam.

Serve for morning coffee or afternoon tea.

Dessert Crêpes

Dessert crêpes have been served with style and flair in high-class restaurants around the world for many years. They look most spectacular as they are flambéed in a special pan over a spirit burner beside your dining table. But do not be put off by this flamboyant presentation. Dessert crêpes are really quite simple and relatively cheap to make—it's the time it takes to make them for which you pay those high restaurant prices!

Dessert crêpes are filled with a variety of exotic, often liqueur-laced fruit fillings. They are usually flambéed in brandy, rum or a rich liqueur just before serving. If you do not possess an attractive flambé pan for flambéing at the dining table, then do it in the kitchen—the crêpes will taste just as good.

Dessert crêpes may also be layered with delicious fillings and served as a gâteau.

There are some delicious recipes for sweet dessert batters in this chapter, but you can also use the plain batters as the fillings are sweet. Why not experiment for yourself?

Apple Pancakes Longueville

Makes 12 pancakes, serves 6

Batter:
125 g (1 cup) plain or all-purpose flour
pinch of salt
30 g (1 tablespoon) caster sugar
finely grated rind of 1 orange
1 egg
1 egg yolk
2 tablespoons melted unsalted butter
250 ml (1 cup) milk
30 g (¼ cup) blanched almonds, finely chopped

Filling:
6 dessert apples, Jonathans or similar
finely grated rind and juice of ½ orange
finely grated rind and juice of ½ lemon
4 tablespoons apricot jam
200 ml (1 small jar) thickened cream
¼ teaspoon ground cinnamon
1 tablespoon melted unsalted butter
icing sugar for sifting
chopped pistachio nuts for decoration

Batter: Prepare batter as for Basic Pancakes (page 13), adding the caster sugar to the sifted flour and the orange rind with the egg. Allow to stand for 30 minutes, then add chopped almonds just before cooking the pancakes.

Filling: Cut apples into quarters and remove peel and core. Cut apple quarters into thick slices and place in a heavy pan with orange and lemon rind and juices and jam. Cover and stew gently until tender, thick and pulpy. If necessary, remove lid and evaporate juices.

Whip cream, add cinnamon and mix together gently.

To finish: When ready to finish pancakes, and not before, fold whipped cream into apple pulp. Divide apple and cream mixture between the pancakes, spread smoothly, then fold each pancake into quarters. Arrange pancakes, overlapping, in a buttered, ovenproof serving dish and brush with melted butter.

Place pancakes in a hot oven at 220°C (425°F) for 5–10 minutes, until heated through.

Serve immediately sifted with icing sugar and sprinkled with pistachio nuts.

Apricot Crêpes
Serves 6

12 crêpes
1 × 825 g (26 oz) can apricot halves
2 oranges
30 g (1 tablespoon) unsalted butter.
6 tablespoons desiccated or shredded coconut
¼ cup Grand Marnier

Make crêpes according to directions for French Crêpes (page 13).

Drain apricots, measure 250 ml (1 cup) apricot juice and pour into a flambé pan.

Grate rind of oranges finely and add to juice in pan. Remove skin from oranges with a small serrated knife, slice oranges thinly or cut into segments and put aside for decoration.

Add butter to pan and heat until butter is melted.

Divide apricots between crêpes, sprinkle with coconut and fold both sides over. Place filled crêpes in the hot sauce in the pan. Heat sauce until boiling, then add the Grand Marnier and ignite. Spoon the sauce over the crêpes until the flame burns out.

Serve immediately, decorated with orange slices.

Cherry Ripe Crêpes
Serves 6

12 crêpes
Filling:
1 × 425 g (14 oz) can cherries *or* 500 g (1 lb) stewed fresh cherries
caster sugar for sprinkling
300 ml (1 carton) cream
pinch of ground cinnamon

Prepare the crêpe batter and make crêpes as directed in French Crêpes recipe (page 13).

Filling: Drain and stone the cherries.

To finish: Place 1 tablespoon cherries on each crêpe and roll up in a cigar shape. Reserve a few for decoration. Sprinkle caster sugar into a large, shallow, ovenproof serving dish and arrange crêpes neatly in a single layer. Sprinkle with more caster sugar and place in a hot oven at 220°C (425°F) for 4–5 minutes to heat through.

Meanwhile, bring the cream and cinnamon to the boil in a saucepan and pour half over the hot cherry crêpes.

Serve hot, decorated with reserved cherries or fresh cherries, if in season, and serve the remaining cinnamon cream in a small jug.

Christmas Crêpes
Serves 6

12 crêpes
Filling:
3 cups Christmas plum pudding
2 eggs, beaten
4 tablespoons ground almonds
4 tablespoons brandy
icing sugar for sifting
Brandy Butter for serving

Prepare crêpes as given in Basic Pancakes recipe (page 13).

Filling: Place plum pudding in a mixing bowl and loosen texture by mixing with a fork. Add beaten eggs, ground almonds and brandy and mix well.

To finish: Divide filling between crêpes and spread in a line over the bottom half of each. Roll up crêpes neatly to a cigar shape and place in a buttered, shallow, ovenproof serving dish.

Place crêpes in a moderately hot oven at 190°C (375°F) for 20–30 minutes until filling is firm and hot.

Serve immediately sifted generously with icing sugar, accompanied with a bowl of Brandy Butter.

Note: A delicious recipe for lovers of Christmas plum pudding for it uses up left-over Christmas pudding in a fascinating gourmet dessert.

Brandy Butter
Serves 6-8

125 g (4 tablespoons) unsalted butter
125 g (½ cup) caster sugar
3 tablespoons brandy

Cream butter until light and fluffy, add sugar and beat well until light and fluffy like whipped cream. Gradually beat in brandy, a teaspoon at a time. Put in a small bowl, cover with clear plastic and chill until firm. Serve with Christmas Crêpes.

Note: To make Rum Butter, substitute rum for brandy and use 125 g (⅔ cup) dark, moist brown sugar in place of caster sugar.

Cottage Cheese Blintzes
Serves 4

8 pancakes, but substitute self-raising flour for plain flour
Filling:
375 g (1¾ cups) cottage cheese
1 egg yolk
2 tablespoons caster sugar
1 teaspoon vanilla essence
60 g (2 tablespoons) unsalted butter for frying
1 teaspoon ground cinnamon
extra 2 tablespoons caster sugar for sprinkling
300 ml (1 carton) sour cream or 1 × 200 g carton natural yoghurt

Prepare pancakes according to Basic Pancakes recipe (page 13), but substitute self-raising flour for plain flour.

Cook pancakes on one side only and turn out on to a clean tea towel or board.

Filling: Mix cottage cheese with egg yolk, caster sugar and vanilla essence.

To finish: Put equal quantities of filling (approximately 1½ tablespoons) in the centre of the cooked side of the pancakes and fold edges over filling, envelope style.

Melt butter in a large pan until it begins to sizzle. Put in 3 or 4 of the blintzes, with joins underneath, and fry until golden on both sides. Remove from pan and drain on absorbent kitchen paper. Keep hot.

Add more butter to pan if necessary and fry remaining blintzes until golden. Sprinkle with cinnamon and sugar and serve immediately, accompanied with sour cream or yoghurt.

Peach Pancake Gâteau

Crêpes Melba
Serves 8

8 crêpes
Sauce:
1 × 450 g (14 oz) can raspberries *or* 1 box fresh raspberries and
2 tablespoons each sugar and water
2 teaspoons cornflour (cornstarch)
1 tablespoon cold water
4 ripe peaches, peeled and sliced
8 scoops vanilla ice cream for filling

Prepare crêpes as directed in French Crêpes recipe (page 13) and keep hot.

Sauce: Put canned raspberries with syrup or fresh raspberries, sugar and water in a clean pan. Bring slowly to the boil, stirring occasionally.

Blend cornflour with 1 tablespoon cold water to a smooth paste. Stir into the raspberries and bring to the boil, stirring continuously until sauce thickens and clears. Add sliced peaches and heat through gently.

To serve, place hot crêpes on individual serving dishes, put a scoop of ice cream on top of each, fold crêpes over and spoon the sauce over. Serve immediately.

Strawberry Pancake Gâteau

Crêpes Parisienne
Serves 6

12 pancakes, but use only 90 g (¾ cup) plain or all-purpose flour
1 tablespoon orange curaçao
Filling:
125 g (4 tablespoons) unsalted butter
60 g (½ cup) icing sugar, sifted
finely grated rind of 2 oranges
juice of 1 orange
3 tablespoons orange curaçao
100 g (1 cup) plain cake crumbs
extra melted butter
icing sugar for sprinkling
125 ml (½ cup) overproof brandy for flaming

Prepare batter according to Basic Pancakes recipe (page 13) but use only 90 g (¾ cup) flour and stir in orange curaçao. Cook crêpes in a small crêpe pan as directed.

Filling: Place butter in a small mixing bowl. Add icing sugar and beat with a wooden spoon until soft and creamy. Add orange rind and juice, orange curaçao and cake crumbs gradually and beat until well combined. Cover and chill until ready to fill crêpes.

To finish: Brush a large baking tray with melted butter and place crêpes on it, in two overlapping rows. Brush crêpes with more melted butter. Place in a slow oven at 150°C (300°F) for 5 minutes.

Remove warm crêpes from oven and spread a tablespoon of filling over each one. Fold crêpes in half then over in half again into the traditional tricorn shape. Place folded crêpes in a warm ovenproof serving dish, sprinkle with icing sugar, cover securely with foil and return to oven to keep warm.

To serve crêpes, heat brandy in a small pan, pour over crêpes and ignite at the table. Alternatively, place a flameproof dish of crêpes over a spirit burner, pour brandy over and ignite it when it starts to simmer. Spoon the juice over the crêpes and serve piping hot.

Fruit Pancakes with Ice Cream

Serves 6

---

12 pancakes/crêpes
Filling:
185 g (1 cup) sultanas
125 ml (½ cup) rum
2 tablespoons water
60 g (½ cup) ground nuts (almonds, hazelnuts or walnuts)
30 g (1 tablespoon) butter
chocolate ice cream for serving

Prepare pancakes as directed in Basic Pancakes recipe or crêpes as in French Crêpes recipe (page 13).

Filling: Place sultanas, rum and water in a saucepan and simmer for 1 minute. Stir in ground nuts and butter, then remove from heat.

To finish: Divide filling between pancakes and fold opposite sides over. Place in a buttered baking dish and bake in a moderately hot oven at 190⁰C (375⁰F) for 10–15 minutes.

Serve pancakes hot on individual dessert plates and top each portion with scoops of chocolate ice cream.

Jubilee Crêpes

Serves 6

---

12 crêpes
1 × 825 g (26 oz) can fruit cocktail
60 g (⅓ cup) brown sugar
125 g (½ cup) unsalted butter
2 bananas, sliced
60 ml (¼ cup) cognac, brandy or orange-flavoured liqueur
extra 60 ml (¼ cup) cognac or brandy to flambé

Prepare crêpes as for Basic Pancakes (page 13).

Drain fruit cocktail and reserve syrup. Melt sugar in a frying pan until golden brown. Add butter and fruit cocktail syrup, bring to the boil and simmer for 2 minutes. Add cognac, brandy or liqueur.

Dip each crêpe into the sauce and fold into quarters. Arrange crêpes, overlapping, in a buttered, flameproof, ovenproof serving dish.

Stir fruit cocktail into sauce and spoon over the crêpes.

Place crêpes in a moderately hot oven at 190⁰C (375⁰F) for 10–15 minutes, until heated through.

At the dining table, pour hot cognac or brandy over the crêpes and ignite. Serve immediately with whipped or pouring cream.

Mandarin Macaroon Crêpes

Serves 6

Batter:
8–10 almond macaroons
155 g (1¼ cups) plain or all-purpose flour
pinch of salt
60 g (2 tablespoons) caster sugar
2 eggs
250 ml (1 cup) milk
1 tablespoon oil
3 tablespoons cream
unsalted butter for cooking

Filling:
1 × 345 g (11 oz) can mandarin oranges
300 ml (1 large jar) thickened cream
2 tablespoons brandy or dry sherry

Batter: Drop almond macaroons, one at a time, on to the revolving blades of a blender, through the hole in the lid, and mix to a biscuit crumb consistency. Empty macaroon crumbs into a bowl.

Place the remaining batter ingredients into the blender and blend until smooth, approximately 45 seconds, stopping and scraping down the sides when necessary. Allow batter to stand for 10–20 minutes then stir in the macaroon crumbs.

Cook crêpes as directed (these cook particularly well on an electric automatic crêpe maker) and keep hot.

Filling: Drain mandarins and reserve syrup. Whip cream until thick, then gently fold mandarins into it. Place mandarin syrup and brandy in a small pan.

To finish: Divide cream filling between crêpes and roll up into cigar shapes.

Place filled crêpes in a single layer in a buttered, shallow, ovenproof serving dish and warm through in a moderate oven at 180°C (350°F) for 10 minutes. Meanwhile, heat syrup until warm, not boiling.

Serve crêpes hot from the oven, accompanied with the warm syrup.

Mango and Melon Crêpes

Serves 8

16 crêpes
Filling:
2 large, ripe mangoes
1 large ripe rock melon (cantaloup)
4 tablespoons kirsch
4 tablespoons brandy or rum
pouring cream or ice cream for serving

Prepare crêpes as for French Crêpes recipe (page 13).

Filling: Peel mangoes, remove fruit from stone and chop fruit coarsely. Place in a bowl.

Cut melon in half lengthways, remove and discard seeds, then cut fruit out with a melon-ball scoop. Add melon to mango and gently fold in the kirsch. Cover and leave to macerate for 30 minutes.

To finish: Divide filling between crêpes, roll up and place in a buttered flambé pan. Pour brandy or rum over, heat over a spirit burner and ignite when liquor is hot.

When flames die out, serve immediately accompanied with pouring cream or ice cream.

Mocha Pancakes

Serves 6

12 pancakes, but substitute 1 tablespoon milk with
1 tablespoon liquid coffee essence
Filling:
60 g (2 oz) plain chocolate, roughly chopped
2 tablespoons warm black coffee
125 g (½ cup) unsalted butter
60 g (¼ cup) ground almonds
15 g (2 teaspoons) caster sugar
1 tablespoon crème de menthe
icing sugar for sprinkling

Make pancakes according to Basic Pancakes recipe (page 13) but substitute 1 tablespoon milk with 1 tablespoon liquid coffee essence.

Filling: Place chocolate and coffee in the top of a double-boiler and melt chocolate in the coffee over gently boiling water. Allow to cool.

Cream butter in a bowl, add the cooled mocha mixture (chocolate and coffee) and beat well. Add the almonds and caster sugar and mix well. Flavour with crème de menthe.

To finish: Spread the filling on to each pancake, roll up and reheat in a hot oven at 200⁰C (400⁰F) for 10 minutes.

Serve hot sprinkled with icing sugar.

Note: A little extra chopped chocolate may be sprinkled over the pancakes before serving.

Orange Glacé Gâteau

Serves 6-8

4 × 18 cm (7 inch) crêpes
Orange glacé:
1 teaspoon gelatine
1 tablespoon cold water
finely grated rind and juice of 1 large orange
4 egg yolks
2 eggs
185 g (¾ cup) caster sugar
185 ml (¾ cup) thickened cream
2 tablespoons orange curaçao
orange slices for decoration

Prepare crêpes according to French Crêpes recipe (page 13).

Orange glacé: Stir gelatine into water in a small heatproof bowl and 'soak' for 5 minutes.

Reserve orange rind and place orange juice in the bowl of an electric mixer. Add egg yolks, eggs and caster sugar and stir over a pan of simmering water until the mixture is lukewarm. Transfer bowl to mixer and beat at high speed until mixture forms a ribbon and holds its shape.

Dissolve gelatine over hot water. Place cream in a bowl and add the gelatine in a thin stream, beating continuously until cream is thick. Gently fold cream mixture and orange rind into egg mixture.

To finish: Sprinkle the 4 crêpes with orange curaçao. Base-line an 18 cm (7 inch) round cake tin with a round of waxed paper and place a crêpe on it. Spread one-third of the orange glacé mixture on top. Continue layering in this manner, finishing with a crêpe. Cover the tin with foil and freeze until set, overnight if possible.

To serve: Loosen gâteau with a round-bladed knife and invert on to a flat serving plate. Place in refrigerator for 45 minutes then serve cut in wedges.

Peach Pancake Gâteau

Serves 6-8

12 pancakes/crêpes
Filling:
4 peaches
125 g (½ cup) caster sugar
½ teaspoon ground cinnamon
2 tablespoons brandy
approx ¾ cup apricot jam
125 g (1 cup) ground almonds
icing sugar for sifting

Prepare pancakes as directed in Basic Pancake recipe or crêpes as in French Crêpes recipe (page 13).

Filling: Peel peaches with a serrated knife, remove stone and cut fruit into segments or slices. Reserve 6–8 of the best peach segments for decoration. Place remaining sliced peaches in a mixing bowl, add caster sugar, cinnamon and brandy and fold together lightly.

To make gâteau: Place a pancake in the centre of an ovenproof serving plate. Arrange 2 or 3 tablespoons sliced peaches on top and drizzle 1 tablespoon juice over. Cover with a second pancake, spread with 2 tablespoons apricot jam and sprinkle 2 tablespoons ground almonds over.

Cover with another pancake and repeat alternate layers of filling and pancakes, finishing with a pancake.

Arrange reserved peach segments on top, sprinkle with ground almonds and sift icing sugar on top. Place in a slow oven at 150°C (300°F) for 15–20 minutes and serve warm, or serve cold.

Cut into wedges and serve with a bowl of whipped cream.

Pineapple Custard Crêpes
Serves 6

12 crêpes/pancakes
Filling:
1 × 450 g (14 oz) can crushed pineapple
2 egg yolks
3 tablespoons sugar
1 tablespoon cornflour (cornstarch)
finely grated rind of 1 lemon
150 ml (approx ⅔ cup) milk
¼ teaspoon vanilla essence
30 g (1 tablespoon) butter
Sauce:
juice from canned pineapple
3 tablespoons brandy or kirsch

Prepare crêpes as directed in French Crêpes recipe or pancakes as in Basic Pancakes recipe (page 13).

Filling: Drain pineapple and reserve juice for sauce.

Place egg yolks, sugar, cornflour and lemon rind in a small mixing bowl and beat with a rotary beater until thick and creamy. Add milk and stir until smooth.

Pour egg yolk mixture into the top of a double-boiler and stir over gently boiling water until mixture thickens. Remove from heat and fold in pineapple, vanilla and butter.

To finish: Divide filling between crêpes and roll up neatly. Place crêpes in a single layer in a shallow, ovenproof serving dish and heat in a moderate oven at 180⁰C (350⁰F) for 10–15 minutes.

Sauce: Place pineapple juice and brandy or kirsch in a saucepan and bring to the boil.

To serve, pour hot sauce over crêpes and serve immediately.

Pineapple Macaroon Pancakes
Serves 6

12 pancakes
Filling:
1 small fresh pineapple
4 tablespoons apricot jam
4 tablespoons crushed macaroons
2 tablespoons kirsch or rum or orange juice
1 tablespoon melted butter
icing sugar for sprinkling
cream for serving

Prepare batter and make pancakes as in Basic Pancakes recipe (page 13).

Filling: Peel pineapple, remove core and dice pineapple finely. Mix pineapple with apricot jam, heat in a pan.

To finish: Spread filling evenly over the pancakes. Sprinkle crushed macaroons and kirsch over the top and fold pancakes in half, then in half again to form triangles.

Put the filled pancakes into a buttered, ovenproof serving dish and brush with melted butter. Place in a hot oven at 220°C (425°F) for 5 minutes or until hot.

Serve hot, sprinkled with icing sugar accompanied with pouring cream.

Soufflé Crêpes with Peaches
Serves 6

12 pancakes/crêpes
Filling:
3 egg whites
⅛ teaspoon cream of tartar
1 tablespoon caster sugar
6 tablespoons peach or strawberry jam
60 g (½ cup) ground hazelnuts
2 cups sliced peaches, fresh or canned
6 scoops ice cream, optional

Make pancakes as directed in Basic Pancakes recipe or crêpes as directed in French Crêpes recipe (page 13).

Filling: Whisk egg whites with cream of tartar until stiff. Whisk in sugar. Add jam and whisk for a few seconds. Gently fold in the ground nuts.

Divide meringue mixture between pancakes and spread over evenly. Roll up the pancakes and place in a single layer in a large, buttered, ovenproof serving dish. Heat in a moderately hot oven at 190°C (375°F) for 15 minutes.

Serve immediately, topped with peaches and a scoop of ice cream.

Slipped Pancake Torte

Makes approximately 14-16, serves 8-10

Batter:
160 g (approx ⅝ cup) unsalted butter
60 g (¼ cup) caster sugar
8 large eggs
90 g (¾ cup) continental flour
500 ml (2 cups) milk
unsalted butter for cooking
Filling:
vanilla icing sugar
60 g (¼ cup) ground almonds
Sugared Berries for serving (page 108)

Batter: Allow butter to soften, then place in the small bowl of an electric mixer with the caster sugar. Separate eggs, add egg yolks to butter and sugar and beat well until light and creamy.

Add sifted flour and stir in gently with a wooden spoon. Gradually stir in the milk. Whisk egg whites until stiff and fold into batter.

To finish: Cook a pancake on one side only, 'slip' out on to a serving plate, and sift generously with vanilla icing sugar. Continue cooking and stacking pancakes in this way, sifting every one generously with vanilla icing sugar.

When completed, sprinkle ground almonds and more vanilla icing sugar on top.

Serve pancake torte hot, cut into segments, accompanied with Sugared Berries.

Note: The name Slipped Pancake Torte comes from a literal translation meaning the pancakes slipped out of the pan.

To make vanilla icing sugar, snip 2 vanilla pods (or beans) into a jar, add 500 g (1 lb) pure icing sugar, stir well, then cover and leave for 1 week for flavour to develop before using.

Continental flour is sold in leading delicatessens.

Sugared Berries
Serves 8

2 boxes ripe raspberries or strawberries
juice of 1 orange
4 tablespoons icing sugar

Hull berries and place in a mixing bowl. Slice strawberries if they are large ones. Sprinkle orange juice and icing sugar over and leave to macerate for at least 30 minutes.

Serve in a polished glass serving bowl with Slipped Pancake Torte (page 107).

Strawberry Pancake Gâteau
Serves 6-8

12 pancakes/crêpes
Filling:
6 tablespoons strawberry jam
finely grated rind and juice of 1 lemon
2 boxes strawberries
2 tablespoons brandy or orange juice
whipped cream for serving

Prepare and cook pancakes according to Basic Pancakes recipe or crêpes as in French Crêpes recipe (page 13).

Filling: Place strawberry jam, lemon rind and juice into a small saucepan and heat gently until combined. Hull strawberries and reserve a few of the best for the top. Slice remaining strawberries into saucepan and bring slowly to simmering point. Remove from heat and stir in brandy or orange juice.

To make gâteau: Place a pancake on an ovenproof plate and spread 2 or 3 tablespoons strawberry mixture on top. Continue layering pancakes, with strawberry mixture between each one, reserving 1 tablespoon strawberry sauce.

Slice or halve reserved strawberries and arrange attractively on top of pancake gâteau and drizzle remaining strawberry sauce on top.

Place in a moderate oven at 180°C (350°F) for 10–15 minutes or until warm, or serve cold.

Serve cut in wedges and accompany with a bowl of whipped cream.

Simple Crêpes Suzette
Serves 4-6

12 crêpes/pancakes
185 g (¾ cup) butter
3 tablespoons sugar
1 cup orange marmalade
finely grated rind of 4 oranges
3 tablespoons orange curaçao or Grand Marnier
extra 2 tablespoons sugar
3 tablespoons brandy

Prepare crêpes as directed in French Crêpes recipe (page 13).

Place butter, 3 tablespoons sugar, marmalade, orange rind and liqueur in a small frying pan and bring slowly to boiling point over a low heat, stirring continuously.

Dip crêpes one at a time into marmalade mixture, then fold each in half, then in half again to form quarters. Place crêpes in a shallow flameproof serving dish and pour remaining marmalade mixture over. Sprinkle extra sugar on top.

Bake crêpes in a hot oven at 200⁰C (400⁰F) for 10–15 minutes, until sugar on top caramelises. Warm brandy, pour over hot crêpes, ignite immediately and serve crêpes flaming.

Quick Crêpes

For some quick dessert crêpes, try these:

Fill warm crêpes with heated, canned pie filling such as apple, apricot, etc., roll up and serve with vanilla ice cream or whipped cream.

Mix some chopped fresh fruit such as Chinese gooseberries, melon, pawpaw, or pear with passionfruit, then fold in some natural yoghurt or thick sour cream. Place in warm crêpes, roll up and serve. A delicious dessert, and it makes a healthy breakfast too.

Fold crêpes in quarters and heat in maple syrup, honey or golden syrup thinned down with orange juice.

Fill warm crêpes with heated fruit mincemeat, roll up and serve with brandy butter or whipped cream.

Sprinkle hot crêpes with lemon juice and caster sugar, roll up and serve immediately with lemon wedges.

Index